PILOT

GEORGE PALMER

PILOT

SURVIVING A CAREER IN AVIATION

… in dedication to my wife, Melissa (Liss)

First published in 2024 by George Palmer

© George Palmer 2024
The moral rights of the author have been asserted

All rights reserved. Except as permitted under the *Australian Copyright Act 1968* (for example, a fair dealing for the purposes of study, research, criticism or review), no part of this book may be reproduced, stored in a retrieval system, communicated or transmitted in any form or by any means without prior written permission.

All inquiries should be made to the author.

A catalogue entry for this book is available from the National Library of Australia.

ISBN: 978-1-923225-20-6

Book production and text design by Publish Central
Cover design by Pipeline Design

The paper this book is printed on is certified as environmentally friendly.

Disclaimer: The material in this publication is of the nature of general comment only, and does not represent professional advice. It is not intended to provide specific guidance for particular circumstances and it should not be relied on as the basis for any decision to take action or not take action on any matter which it covers. Readers should obtain professional advice where appropriate, before making any such decision. To the maximum extent permitted by law, the author and publisher disclaim all responsibility and liability to any person, arising directly or indirectly from any person taking or not taking action based on the information in this publication.

CONTENTS

Foreword ix
In Memory of Lost Friends xiii
Introduction 1

1 Living the Dream *1949–2022* 5
2 Early Days *1965–1972* 9
3 Charter Pilot *1972–1977* 29
4 Heavy Time *1977–1978* 59
5 Connair Darwin *1979–1981* 69
6 Ansett Take-over *1981* 81
7 Jets at Last *1982* 95
8 Polynesian Airlines *1985* 107
9 Pilots' Dispute *1989* 115
10 Initial Command *1990* 119
11 Line Captain *1990–1995* 129
12 Flying the Boeing 747 *1995–2001* 139
13 A Year in Singapore *1998–1999* 147
14 Back to Ansett *1999–2001* 153
15 Back to Singapore *2001–2011* 157
16 Flying the Line *2001–2011* 163
17 Out of Retirement *2012–2022* 179
18 COVID *2020–2022* 193

Appendices:

A	The Bristol B170 Freighter	197
B	The De Havilland DH114 Heron	200
C	The Fokker F27 Friendship	203
D	The Boeing 727	206
E	The Boeing 737	208
F	The Boeing 747	211
G	The GAF Nomad	215
H	Light Aircraft	218

Acknowledgements	223
Aviation Definitions	225

FOREWORD

George Palmer is a pilot of wide and varied experience in aviation, having commanded the smallest of general aviation aircraft types to the largest airline aircraft in the world.

He began his career flying single-engine light aircraft in the unforgiving heat and pervading dust of outback Australia, followed by an extensive tenure in the airline industry. This ultimately led to George training pilots for long-range international operations on the mighty queen of the skies – the Boeing 747.

George is one of those rare individuals who truly have an affinity with the air. He has amassed in excess of 26,000 flying hours and has flown well over a million passengers to their destinations. The trust they placed in him was, indeed, not misplaced.

In this book, George will humbly present to you, the reader, his treasured twenty-one-year association with Ansett Airlines. He reflects upon the bonds that were forged in the cockpit with the men and women who shared the interminable hours of turbulence; the negotiation of thunderstorms that stretched for hundreds of miles; flights that often included the uncertainties of fuel, endurance, and destination weather conditions. How different it is today, where successful arrivals are virtually assured by the use of GPS and automated flight and landing system technology.

George presents the vagaries of operating grossly underpowered light aircraft prior to the use of turbo charging, through the period of flying 'the classic' 747 into the infamous Kai Tak airport at Hong Kong, and onto the sophisticated 747-400 with Singapore Airlines.

After an exemplary career and seeing the dawn through too many cockpit windows, the time has arrived for George to come home. He has returned to his grassroots where it all began for him, instructing those who wish to unravel the wondrous mysteries of flight.

It is a privilege for me to introduce this book to you, with the wish that the wonders and mysteries of flight may, through one man's experiences, be shared with you.

Captain Ken Broomhead OAM
B747 Fleet Manager Ansett International,
Chief Pilot Tiger Airways

*Emergencies you train for
almost never happen.
It is the ones you can't train for
that kill you.*

Ernest K Gann, author of *Fate is the Hunter*

IN MEMORY OF LOST FRIENDS

† **Peter Benton, Piper Chieftain, VH-MBK**
30 March 1978
Engine fire on take-off from Melbourne Airport, at maximum weight, at night and in poor weather. Crashed attempting return. Wooded area adjacent to runway 27, Melbourne Airport.

† **John Fleming, Cessna 182Q, VH-UDM**
10 May 1978
Attempted to avoid a thunderstorm, experienced navigation difficulties with a faulty radio compass and no distance measuring equipment. Hit high ground at night. Seven miles east of Tooraweenah, New South Wales.

† **Jim O'Connell, De Havilland DH84 Dragon, VH-AGC**
15 December 1979
The vintage twin-engine biplane suffered an engine failure shortly after take-off. Loss of control and stall during turn-back in strong gusty northerly winds. RAAF Base Point Cook, Victoria.

† **John Lindridge, B58 Baron, VH-CTU**
12 March 1983
Flew into the ground on a night departure. Cause: unknown, possible incapacitation. 14 miles south of Wynyard, Tasmania.

† **Peter Lemon, Mitsubishi MU2B, VH-MLU**
24 May 1983
After climbing to 16,000 feet, dived vertically into the ground. Cause: unknown, suspected severe icing conditions led to loss of control. One mile east of Bargo, New South Wales.

† **Bill Surh, Cessna 402, Air Ambulance, VH-RED**
3 September 1986
Engine failure during take-off. With marginal performance on the remaining engine, loss of control trying to avoid power lines over the Tullamarine Freeway. Essendon, Melbourne.

† **Jim Millar, De Havilland DHC-6 Twin Otter, P2-MBI**
12 July 1995
In-flight explosion and fire leading to loss of control. Unauthorised kerosene illegally loaded by a passenger spilt and started a fire. Papua New Guinea.

† **Terry Otway, Brumby R600, 24-7322 (RAA register)**
9 April 2016
Entered unintentional spin during training exercise and failed to recover. Crashed into a paddock near Lancefield, Victoria. Student also killed.

† **David and Jan Maddern, Jabaru-400, VH-EDJ**
28 July 2023
Mid-air collision during take-off, collided with Piper Pawnee VH-PTA which was overshooting a crossing runway, having told David he was holding short. Caboolture, Queensland.

INTRODUCTION

History records man's first powered flight as credited to the Wright brothers on 17 December 1903 at Kitty Hawk, North Carolina in the US. Orville Wright successfully completed a 12-second flight over a distance of 260 metres. Hardly earth-shattering, and today even disputed by some history buffs. It is not part of my narrative to enter the dispute, as much of it depends on definition. It is enough to say the first decade of the 20th century was the beginning of a new occupation of pilotage.

Many names from this period were to become famous – Louis Bleriot, Samuel Cody, Graham Bell, Glen Curtiss and many more. Early aeroplanes were flimsy crude affairs and man's initial attempts at controlling a flying machine were fraught with danger. Crashes seemed par for the course and the fatality rate was horrendous. It was during World War I, 1914–1918, that aviation began to make giant leaps forward. Simple observation machines, often held in ridicule by the hierarchy, quickly transformed into efficient killing machines. They were still incredibly dangerous to the pilot with casualties in training running on par with operational losses. The career life spans of military pilots were often measured in weeks.

Little was known about hypoxia at high altitudes, no parachutes were worn and pilot safety devices in general were non-existent. No such thing as brakes or protection from every aviator's worst fears, in-flight fire, as well as the weather. Little was known about advanced aerodynamics such as flutter, and some machines had questionable handling qualities. The English Sopwith Camel with its rotary engine and giant wooden propeller had some interesting gyroscopic issues. Turning to the left away from the torque of the spinning engine tended to be sluggish and raised the nose. The sudden loss of airspeed could lead to a stall. To the right, it tightened the turn and lowered the nose. Some pilots wanting to turn to the left simply went the long way around through 270 degrees. For those who mastered this quirky machine, it became deadly in a close quarter dogfight. The Camel had the highest number of kills for any aircraft during that conflict, some 1294 enemy aircraft. Still, additional facts tell a sobering story. There were 413 Camel pilots killed in combat and 385 died from non-combat accidents. A modern health and safety department would have a pink fit.

Following World War I, civilian aviation really took off. From humble beginnings to within ten years, giant lumbering bi-planes like the Handley-Page HP42 flew regular services to the colonies. Beautiful four-engine flying boats flew around the world in art-deco style and luxury. Some services had equal crew to passengers and only the wealthy could afford to fly. Then in the mid to late thirties, the more efficient monoplanes began to appear. One of the most revolutionary was the Douglas DC-2. Improved as the DC-3, one could argue this aircraft alone brought air travel to the general population.

World War II was the next major turning point. There is nothing like a good old-fashioned war to speed up development – and speed up was an understatement. By the war's end, bi-plane fighters had been replaced by jets with advanced piston-engine aircraft in between. The Germans had discovered the advantages of swept wings, high-lift devices and rocket technologies to name a few. Considering this was over a mere five-year period, the advances were truly remarkable.

Following the war, civilian aviation had its turn, although not without some major failures. The English Comet, the world's first jet airliner, paid a terrible price discovering the finer points of pressurisation systems. The time it took to discover the cause of several crashes gave the American aircraft industry time to catch up. The lead made by Boeing with the 707 was the beginning of a sad decline in British leadership in airliner design. It was not helped by the English trying to extend the life of large flying boats such as the Saro Princess. And who could forget the mighty Bristol Brabazon? With coupled piston engines (eight in four nacelles), it was a commercial disaster.

The fifties and sixties produced more efficiencies and after a brief love affair with turboprop aircraft (basically a jet turbine driving a propeller), the jets became the norm for long distance travel. The seventies and eighties saw the development of high by-pass engines producing more power for much improved fuel consumption. The so-called 'wide bodies' with dual isle cabins and larger passenger capacity carrying aircraft appeared, including the iconic Boeing 747. Flying was now available to people of modest means, so passenger numbers trebled on long haul routes.

Some could argue that from the eighties to the present, not much has changed but looks can be deceiving. More efficient engines giving giant leaps in power and software advances such as EEC (Electronic Engine Control) assisted the pilots with thrust management. The Pratt and Whitney JT-8 engines producing 15,000 lbs of thrust on the early 727 and 737 aircraft are hair-dryers compared to the Rolls Royce Trent on the Boeing 777 producing 100,000 lbs of thrust. Sophisticated computers and fly-by-wire flight controls have replaced hydraulics and cables. It is true we seem to be at a pause with speed, as modern jets of today are still cruising around Mach. 85, the same speed of the sixties' aircraft.

We have the technology to go faster as proven by the British- and French-designed Concorde of Mach 2 fame. The trouble is the fuel burn to achieve these speeds, let alone the development costs, are prohibitive. Most advances now appear to be in the software department to such an extent that automation will replace pilots altogether in the next fifty years. Drones are starting to be the weapon of choice as witnessed by the latest conflict in Ukraine. Whether or not the public will accept pilotless aircraft remains to be seen. Personally, if I am still around, I'd prefer to go by train, as the best computer ever made, despite many weaknesses, is what we find between our ears. Aviation is safer than ever, but the fast-moving dynamics require thinking out of the box sometimes and I have yet to see a computer that can do this.

Piloting has been a wonderful occupation, but it is not easy to forge a stable career. It has many pitfalls, requires dedication and hard work but like all things with such demands, it is immensely satisfying. There is nothing quite like soaring with the eagles.

My intention for this book is to tell would-be aviators what the real journey is all about, not the one produced in the glossy brochures. If laypeople find it interesting, all the better.

1
LIVING THE DREAM
1949–2022

Flying is more than a sport and more than a job,
flying is pure passion.
Adolf Galland

On 2 December 2006 at ten minutes to midnight, I lifted off runway 02 centre at Changi Airport, flying a Boeing 747-400 registered 9V-SPD of Singapore Airlines. The destination was Paris LFPG in the world of aviation or Charles de Gaulle as called by the travel industry. With me in the cockpit was a relief Captain and two co-pilots, Captain S. Pathy and F/0s S. Tay and S. Tan. With the propensity to introduce each other by their surnames, I was already uncertain with the two co-pilots as to who was Tay and who was Tan. With a planned flight time of 13 hours and 15 minutes, I was sure to have it sorted by the time we arrived at our destination.

At this time Singapore had 44 passenger 747s and over a dozen of the freighter version so it was not unusual to fly with a crew for the first time. On arrival at the briefing room, they all seemed unusually happy to see me – this was Singapore's last 747 flight to Paris as the route was being taken over by the new Airbus 380. The captain rostered for this historical occasion was the Fleet Manager himself but at the last moment he had to attend an important company meeting. I was called out so late in the proceedings that the crew were still expecting the boss and seemed relieved it was now a harmless Australian expat.

I have kept the first page of the flight plan, a habit I formed as a back-up record for my logbook. Since retiring, most have been thrown out but this one survives. It records a push-back time of 1607 UTC or seven minutes past midnight Singapore local time. We were scheduled out at 1550 so I was 17 minutes late. The reasons for this have long been forgotten but the plan did have a BOBCAT slot time ten minutes after schedule. BOBCAT was an acronym for Bay of Bengal Crossing Arrival Time. With the large amount of traffic crossing the Bay of Bengal to the Indian subcontinent at this time of night, aircraft were assigned 'slots' based on their arrival time on the other side of the bay. Seven minutes over this time would indicate a renewed slot probably caused by a 'runner', a late boarding passenger. The flight was full or close to it, looking at the take-off weight, including 160 tons of fuel.

As I had to complete the approach and landing in Paris, I took the first rest utilising a bunk bed just behind the cockpit. In the years as a 747 captain, I rarely gained more than a few hours of quality sleep. The bunk was noisy and next to one of the upper deck toilets. Adding to the noise was the cockpit door alarm every time a flight attendant requested entry.

Joining the duty crew again over the Indian–Pakistan border I settled in for the remainder of the flight. Laypeople often ask, "How do you fill in your time when on autopilot?" The short answer is we can be surprisingly busy. There is no hiding the fact there are times of relative inactivity, but it can be the opposite at times. There are sensitive borders that require military clearances as well as civilian ones. Fuel and weather require constant watching and planning escape routes over high terrain in the event of decompression. Winds and turbulence often demand a change in altitude, and this is complicated by other traffic and speed control requirements from Air Traffic Control. The airspace through Afghanistan was another bun fight trying to get into position to gain the optimum level and route. After Afghanistan, and a plethora of 'Stans' countries, this was followed by the Caspian Sea, the Black Sea and into Europe. At this time of year, outside air temperatures would be minus fifty something or even colder. Cold fuel could be a problem trying to avoid fuel icing. We had a choice of either descending into warmer air or going faster. The added speed would increase skin temperatures to warm the fuel but could eat up your reserves. So, there was always something to do, not to mention the charming Singapore cabin crew serving up a constant flow of food and drinks. I had a reputation of having a sweet tooth and the crew would save me some of the first-class desserts. Munching on fruit tarts over the Black Sea at four in the morning was an unusual side benefit of long-haul flying.

After crossing most of Europe, we were handed over from 'Rine', the German controllers, to the French air traffic system and given our STAR (Standard Instrument Arrival) for runway 26 Left into Paris. Our schedule arrival was 0525 UTC or 07.25am local time and at this time of year, daylight was an hour away. So having taken off in the dark, here we were more than 13 hours later still in the dark. I remember the French countryside in the moonlight with flat layers of mist and patches of fog. Lines of car headlights like columns of luminous ants slowly snaked towards the city ahead of us. Normal commuters were beginning their day whereas we were just finishing ours. Despite the areas of fog and mist the airport ATIS (Airport Traffic and Information Service, an automated actual weather broadcast) indicated clear skies and calm winds although it was a cold 5 degrees Celsius. Cleared for the ILS (Instrument Landing System) for runway 26 Left we were told to contact the tower.

With a friendly "Bonjour", we were cleared to land. After landing, the French ground controllers, all sounding like Inspector Clouseau from the Pink Panther, politely gave us directions to the gate.

Clearing customs, futuristic glass tunnels led us to the crew bus and on to the Meridian Hotel. The Meridian was opposite the Le Palais des Congres convention hall and railway station, and only a short walk to the Arc de Triomphe and the equally famous Champs-Elysée shopping area. The Singapore crew loved to shop there and would pay a small fortune for designer goods, very much a status symbol in their culture. The crew always looked glamorous in their uniforms, and being young and beautiful certainly attracted the attention from bystanders. With a crew of 22, arriving at the hotel together always caused a log jam towards the check-in counter. The long line of beautiful girls caught the attention of a waiting American Cargo crew. "Sweet Jesus," the captain whispered to me as I drew alongside him. I whispered back, "Somebody has to do it!" which caused his co-pilots to laugh out loud.

On reaching the check-in desk it quickly became apparent the room was still in the name of the Fleet Manager and this seemed to cause the receptionist some stress. With much arm waving and a few "Sacre bleus", this theatrical drama was quickly resolved. It turned out the room for our boss was a suite complete with champagne and a large fruit basket. I decided to share the ill-gotten gains with the crew and in turn the cabin manager asked if I would like to join them on a tour of the city. With 48 hours before departure back to Singapore, it was decided we would meet after a short four-hour sleep around midday. On reaching the room I drew the curtains open and gazed out at the views which included the Eiffel Tower in the distance. The sun was now coming up above the terraced roofs with their quaint attic windows and multitude of chimney stacks. I thought, 'How the hell did I get a job like this, and imagine being well-paid to do it'. Well, it wasn't easy.

2
EARLY DAYS
1965–1972

Believe you can and you're already halfway there.
Teddy Roosevelt

I have read many autobiographies that commonly present the author with a clear recollection of childhood happenings. To my dismay, my earliest memories can at best be described as a jumbled kaleidoscope of images, with only a few events that are etched in any detail, in part due to the constant relocation of my family to Royal Air Force (RAF) bases throughout the world, including stays in Germany and Singapore.

I was born on 14 May 1949, at the Princess Mary's Royal Air Force Hospital, located on the RAF base in Halton, Buckinghamshire, England, home to the No. 1 School of Technical Training (aircraft engineering school) and the RAF Apprenticeship scheme. My father, a serving RAF Officer and pilot, was retrained as an Air Traffic Controller after the war. His first wife, Jessie, was killed during a German air raid on London. He later met my mother, a

Kine-Theodolite operator with a 3.7 anti-aircraft gun battery in the defence of London.

The Kine-Theodolite was an odd-looking device, resembling a cross between a rangefinder and a telescope. Through a view finder, the operator tracked and filmed the target, later reviewed to check firing accuracy.

My father died of natural causes in 2001 and my mother, up until her passing in August 2021, would suffer from debilitating nervous reactions to any loud noises. I was with her the day she died, sharing a bottle of champagne on the end of her hospital bed – I think the nurses were mortified but it was at her request. She knew she was dying and wanted to say goodbye. She was very stoic in that English way and said, "Don't make a fuss, just pour me a drink."

It is hard to imagine what my parents went through during this terrible period of history and neither would voluntarily discuss it. In recent years, my mum opened up a little more. She described that after a practice shoot, they would often be on the receiving end of a fly-past by the operating aircraft. On one occasion, the friendly aircraft with which they were exercising completed a low, high-speed pass only to collide with a raised gun barrel. The aircraft suffered a severely damaged tailplane and slowly rolled over to crash into the sea nearby. I have traced this tragedy to a Hawker Henley Mark 1 target-tug (L3301) on 26 September 1942. Both crew members were killed.

I was born into this very military family as the second of five boys and for some reason, I was the only one who wanted to become a pilot. This ambition was humoured at first, but my obsession became more apparent as time went on and I never wavered. One thing that went against this interest was a deep fear of helicopters. My parents have recounted that I would run inside the house bawling my eyes out on hearing a helicopter. My older brother, Ian, would remain outside and calmly observe its passage with interest. He showed no concern whatsoever. The helicopters of the time were crude affairs compared to the sophisticated machines of today. The Bristol Sycamore used by the Royal Air Force (RAF) had wooden rotor blades that would loudly slap the air. Depending on the wind direction, they could often be heard before being seen. The deep earthy 'wop wop' of their blades would rattle the windows and be enough to turn me to tears. I still have a deep suspicion of any flying machine that must beat the air to death.

I have never been in a helicopter and intend to keep it that way. When we are playing the tourist, there is often a helicopter ride in the package and this causes my wife some embarrassment when I refuse to go. "They all know you are a pilot, and it makes you look silly," she says. I am the first to admit that this fear is puzzling but I cannot help it. A good friend calls them "angry palm-trees", a perfect description. Aeroplanes, on the other hand, have fascinated me for as long as I can remember.

Once, as a six-year-old, I pedalled my tricycle to the local RAF station and climbed over an emergency access gate to wave to the pilots. The aircraft were Gloster Meteors and belonged to a local night fighter squadron – it taxied right alongside the gate. To my great delight, the pilots all waved back. After I was apprehended by the Military Police, my father was summoned to secure my release and the Sergeant in charge said, "Sir, I think we have a flyer in this one." My father obtained some mileage from this story and it is one of the earliest events I can remember.

I also recall sailing through the Suez Canal, as well as my first visits to India where my father grew up as the son of a Naval Officer. I had a real fear of my grandfather, a no-nonsense and extremely strict man in that militaristic way, complete with the shiniest shoes imaginable. On 31 May 1918, he was awarded the Distinguished Service Order when serving as head engineer on the destroyer HMS Fairy. His ship successfully rammed and sank a German U-boat, UC-75. Previously, he served on the battleship HMS Queen Elizabeth during the Dardanelles campaign, shelling the beaches for the ANZAC landings. He seemed to resent my father's decision to join the Air Force and not the Royal Navy. My obvious interest in a similar career was viewed with thinly disguised indifference. Grandpa believed 'real men went to sea.'

I clearly remember exotic places like Aden on the Yemen Peninsula with the Officers' Mess cleaning ladies carrying tins of 'Vim' balanced on their heads, as well as the goat-filled streets of Crater City. 'Crater', officially named Seera but known even by the locals as 'Kraytar', was a city built within an ancient volcano rising out of the Shamsan Mountains directly behind the Aden harbour. The RAF had a large base there called Khormaksar. The British military finally left Yemen in November 1976.

My school years in Singapore also stand out due to the difficulties I had in keeping up with the syllabus. The constant moves resulted in my falling behind in class. This eroded my confidence to the point that I fell further behind. Teachers wrote uncomplimentary reports with statements like 'must try harder' and 'needs to concentrate more.' All efforts to hide these reports from my parents proved a dismal failure.

When my father was posted back to England we moved to Cornwall and lived in the married quarters at RAF St Eval, another famous wartime base. My father was posted to nearby St Mawgan. Here, aged 14, I joined 781 Squadron of the Air Training Corps, the highlight being summer camps where the opportunity existed to fly as passengers under 'air experience'. I flew in Handley-Page Hastings, Avro Ansons and an Armstrong Whitworth Argosy from Thorney Island.

One unforgettable experience was a flying lesson in a Slingsby T21 Glider on 7 October 1963 (serial number WT868), with instructor Pilot Officer A. Hook. We were winched into the air from St Eval and I marvelled at the neat square fields with their straight hedgerows. The only disappointment was being back on the ground after what seemed like only a few minutes.

A month later, I scrounged a five-hour flight from St Mawgan in an Avro Shackleton WR977 of 201 Squadron; this actual aircraft still exists, preserved by the Newark Air Museum in the UK, one of only a handful to survive. The purpose of the patrol was to monitor Russian trawlers which were in reality highly sophisticated spy ships monitoring the RAF. As a 14-year-old cadet, I found this a great adventure. The pilots said things like "jolly good show" and personified my boyhood images of pilots from my reading of *Biggles* by Captain W.E. Johns. My desire to fly was set in concrete after these impressionable events.

During August 1964, when I was 15, my father left the Air Force and we migrated to Australia under the 'ten-pound Pom' scheme. This program of the Australian Government, for the cost of £10, financed English migrants to Australia. We arrived on the migrant ship SS Fairsky six weeks later, docking at Outer Harbour in Adelaide. Once again, we had passed through the Suez Canal and stopped over in Ceylon and Fremantle in Western Australia. I was now 13 months above the average age of my classmates at my Adelaide school and had difficulties settling into the Australian system. I somehow passed the Intermediate Certificate and moved on to my Leaving year. My main weakness now was mathematics – the teachers took great delight in telling me I would never be a pilot without high grades in maths.

I joined the Australian Air Training Corps with Number 13 Flight at Penfield and quickly gained valuable experience in the Link Trainer. Crude by modern standards but still classified as a simulator, it was especially useful to learn the basics of Instrument Flying. Instrument Flying is learning how to fly without reference to the ground, control maintained by indications and instruments inside the cockpit only. In the early days, it was called 'blind flying.' The main difficulty is learning how to ignore 'false sensations' due to the limitations of the human body due to gravitational forces.

Flight Lieutenant Doug Orchard, a war-time pilot with the Distinguished Flying Cross, took a shine to me and allowed me unlimited access to the machine. Years later, like most young pilots with a new licence and no instrument rating, I got caught on more than one occasion in bad weather. This basic grounding in the Link provided instrument skills that clearly saved my life. Doug Orchard died before I ever had the chance to thank him, but I have never forgotten his kindness. He was the first person I had ever met who believed in my dream.

At the age of 16 I finally reached the minimum age to learn to fly; the main obstacle now was the high cost of 5 pounds, 10 shillings an hour for the lesson. My parents agreed to let me work after school as a 'casual' with the usual proviso of "not letting it interfere with your schoolwork." I was lucky enough to obtain work straightaway at the local branch of Woolworths. The family, in the meantime, had moved into a new house at Para Hills overlooking Parafield Aerodrome, the runway visible from my bedroom window. All seemed to be falling nicely into place.

Parafield, as the 'secondary airport' for Adelaide is a General Aviation hub. In the sixties, it had no runways as such and was not much more than a big paddock. The hangars and supporting infrastructure were placed in a simple 'L' on its northern boundary with the control tower at the apex of the 'L'. The tower dates to pre-war times and has commanding views over the entire field. Modified over the years, the building still has that old-world charm and retains its 1930s feel. Parafield in the sixties was designated 'an all-over-field' – aircraft took off and landed in fixed directions or runways, but they consisted only of white threshold markers on the grass. Following take-offs and landings you were required to be to the right of any existing traffic. On landing, you completed a 180 degree turn and backtracked parallel to the landing direction to the threshold prior to vacating onto the concrete apron. This proved to be a simple system that could handle a surprising amount of traffic with multiple arrivals simply landing to the right of the aircraft ahead of them.

The Royal Aero Club of South Australia at the time had an ex-RAF Squadron Leader as its Chief Flying Instructor who was known to my father from his Air Force days, so the Club seemed a natural choice. In 1965 the Club's fleet included eight Victa Airtourers, a local design by Chief Designer Henry Millicer from the Government Aircraft Factories (GAF) which won several overseas awards. A low-wing side-by-side seating aircraft, it was powered by a Rolls-Royce O-200A four-cylinder, horizontally opposed engine of 100hp. Well-built and stressed to withstand +9g and -3g, the aircraft was fully aerobatic. In aviation, the stress on an airframe is called Load Factor and is measured in units referred to as 'g.' In level flight, lift is equal to weight and the aircraft would have a load factor of 1g. In a 2g turn the forces would double, giving an 80kg pilot the feeling of weighing 160kg. The design limit for light aircraft in the 'normal' category is 3.8g and they are restricted to non-aerobatic manoeuvres. The Airtourer was obviously built like a brick outhouse and I liked the look of them. I watched them fly over the family home and could not wait to have a lesson.

The great day finally arrived on 1 August 1965 when my father drove me to the club and introduced me to Charles Roper, the Certified Flight Instructor. He was not what I expected. Very tall, over six feet, thin as a rake and softly spoken to the point of being barely audible. A former Armstrong Whitworth Argosy pilot, he was flying cadets on my camp at Thorney Island. It later turned out I was a passenger on one of his final flights before leaving the Air Force – a small world. We established an immediate rapport, especially when I appeared wearing a crisp white shirt with a tie and called him Sir. I was still very much a 'military brat' and could not imagine calling him anything else.

After signing the paperwork, we walked out to the aircraft, completed the pre-flight checks, and climbed up onto the wing. Sliding back the canopy, I stepped onto the blue vinyl seat and sat down. Mr Roper kept up a constant patter about "watch this" and "don't touch that." In all the excitement I had trouble retaining anything he said. With the canopy slammed shut with a loud thump, we were suddenly sealed into another world of instruments, switches, clicking fuel pumps and other strange electrical noises. Within seconds the propeller began to turn, only to disappear into a great transparent disc as the engine fired. Now with the noise and vibration, I had difficulty hearing Mr Roper's instructions and the confusion to my senses was complete. We waddled awkwardly across the grass and I became aware of how much the aeroplane extended all around me. Unlike driving a car, taxying an aircraft required watching the wings on both sides as well as to the front at the same time.

Something was said on the radio, and with a "You all set, lad?" we were suddenly on our way, noisily accelerating and bouncing over the grass. With a gentle pull on the stick, we rose smoothly up from the ground, which gave the strange sensation of de-accelerating as it fell away. The horizon opened up, revealing a neat patchwork of quilted fields. With a light rocking in the heat turbulence, we climbed slowly skywards. I glanced down at the swaying treetops below, totally intoxicated with the sensation of flight. This is where I wanted to be, and I gave Mr Roper a giant grin of approval. "Did you get that?" he shouted. "Sorry, Sir, could you repeat that please?" I was finally on my way; my life in the air had begun.

It soon became apparent that I could only afford to fly twice a month. Charles Roper considered I would be better off saving up the total amount required and then flying on a more regular basis; after all, I was only 16. Teenagers rarely accept advice and I was no exception. I was determined to proceed as the money became available.

I worked hard at Woolworths and had the staff restrooms and canteen looking ready for a queen's inspection. Promoted to the deep freeze section, I soon had that re-sorted and was elevated to the shop floor to deal with the dairy section. I worked Wednesday, Thursday and Friday nights and even managed some cleaning duties every second Saturday. School homework increased to three hours a night and Private Pilot theory studies via correspondence commenced in earnest. Even with this workload, I found time for a girlfriend; such is the power of youth.

Due to irregular and infrequent lessons I had several Instructors – their individual techniques varied but despite this, I made satisfactory progress. One Instructor was Elizabeth Mariner, who was four months pregnant with her first child. I liked her instantly. She once annotated the flight documents as two and a half people on board, which appealed to my very English sense of humour. It was with Elizabeth I flew 'circuits and bumps' – the art of learning how to take-off and land.

After she became "too pregnant," my new Instructors included Mr Terry Haines, a man who looked more suited to being a professional rugby player. Strongly built with a bull neck, he was, nevertheless, amicable. He was very Australian in his manner and somewhat exasperated, said, "For Christ-sake, stop calling me Sir. My name is Terry, mate!"

After half an hour of circuits, he directed me back towards the apron. I suddenly felt a knot in my stomach; to me, the landings had been okay, with only one skip or two and I could not understand why we were returning. He asked me to park the brakes but leave the engine running. He slid back the canopy and climbed out onto the wing. Leaning over, he fastened his now empty harness and shouted over the noise of the engine, "Just do one circuit and try not to stuff it up." With that, Terry Mate jumped onto the grass and walked off without even looking back. He was sending me solo!

I sat there like a rabbit in the headlights for a minute, and then with a thumping heart, I closed the canopy and called the tower for another circuit. Taxing back to the runway, I kept looking at the empty seat beside me and still could not believe it. I felt I was getting close but expected at least two more lessons. I very carefully went through the take-off checks, double-checked everything once more and called the Tower. With a take-off clearance, I pushed the throttle open, kept it straight with rudder and tried to concentrate on the rapidly increasing airspeed. Without the weight of the instructor, the aeroplane leaped into the air before I felt it should. Gingerly allowing it to accelerate, I eased into a climb and I was flying solo!

As I turned downwind it occurred to me that this was all very well and good, but there was the small detail of getting back down again! I suddenly felt very vulnerable. Turning onto the base leg, which is 90 degrees to the final alignment, I felt high and gained some excess speed as the runway slid onto the nose. Crossing the runway threshold, I was still a little high and fast but managed a respectable landing and taxied in triumph to the apron. Awaiting my arrival were Terry and Charles Roper, who promptly cut my tie in half with a pair of scissors – an aviation tradition. The trophy, one of my father's favourites that I had borrowed, was pinned onto the notice board with congratulations all round. I had achieved solo after 11 hours of flying over five and a half months. Hardly a cracking pace but at 16, I was the youngest to solo at the Club.

Some years later, another 16-year-old went solo amid much publicity in the local paper and was declared the youngest pilot in South Australia to achieve this claim. I took this as an early lesson in not believing everything you read in the newspapers.

Over the next few months, I worked hard at school and tried to keep up, but it was obvious I was not destined for academic greatness and re-aligned my goals to just survive. The flying lessons continued to be dictated by money, or more accurately, the lack of it. In 1966 Australia converted to decimal currency, and the flying rate became $11.50 an hour. Earning half that a week, I felt very frustrated and managed to earn some extra money by cleaning aircraft belonging to the local Piper dealer. The engineer in charge, Jimmy Jenkins, would yell out, "Keep it up if you want to be a pilot." Somehow, I think he enjoyed seeing a future pilot on his back covered in oil. Overall, he treated me very fairly and paid cash up front.

I was now learning advanced manoeuvring including spinning. Years later I was to discover that the Airtourer was a poor spin trainer.

For the reader without aviation experience, this might be an opportunity to explain the black art of basic aerodynamics. If we were to take a cross-section of an aircraft's wing, the upper surface is curved. This curved shape is called 'camber'. When projected through the air, the air going over the top of the curved surface has further to travel compared to the air under the flat bottom. This results in the air on the top of the wing going faster in relation to the air underneath. Speeding up the air in this fashion causes a drop in pressure. With more pressure now below the wing, the difference in pressure creates lift and the wing rises. This basic principle is applied to all the control surfaces.

To turn an aeroplane, simple moving panels called ailerons increase the camber on one wing and work in reverse on the opposite side by decreasing it. With one wing now producing more lift than the other, the aircraft will roll. Balancing with the rudder, we are now turning. The rudder works exactly like a ship's rudder and is operated with left and right foot pedals. The tail is also equipped with moving controls called elevators. Pushing forward on the control column, the elevators move down increasing the camber on the tailplane raising the tail and lowering the nose into a dive. It goes without saying this description is basic, and the variations and combinations are many. In jet aircraft, swept-back wings allow high speed at the expense of lift. To keep landing speeds sensible, high lift devices slats and flaps are used on both the front (leading edge) and various flaps are positioned on the back of the wing (trailing edge). All moving tailplanes and lift-dumping devices, called spoilers, add to the complexity.

This is why aeroplanes are so interesting – they become three-dimensional machines with almost life-like qualities and seem to have their own personalities. Pilots fly the wing, developing a feel for their machines, knowing where the lift can be increased and more importantly knowing where not to go to destroy it. Losing the smooth laminar flow of lift, the wing is considered 'stalled' and may as well not be there. A stalled wing needs room in the vertical to achieve the creation of lift again. For this reason, stalling close to the ground is very unwise. If one wing stalls before the other the aircraft will rotate around the stalled wing and can enter what is known as a spin. During World War II the stall/spin accident rate in training was high, partly due to the aircraft design and partly in the rush to create more aircrew. Today, spin training is no longer compulsory, the popular consensus being that it is dangerous, and more people are killed in training than real events. I disagree, as all aeroplanes can enter a spin, and it seems a good idea to know how to recover.

To enter a spin where the aircraft literally spins around its normal axis pointing straight down, the throttle is first closed. Approaching the stall, full rudder in the direction of spin required is applied, together with full back stick. Standard recovery is to apply full opposite rudder, followed by full forward stick until the rotation stops. A pull-out from the ensuing dive completes the sequence.

The Airtourer was a reluctant host to this manoeuvre and wanted to enter a spiral dive. Entry speed was 60 knots with the nose held just above the horizon. A trick to get into a fully developed spin was, as you rolled over on entry, you gave it a quick jab of opposite aileron. The subsequent rate of rotation was high and restricted to two turns, with much rattling of the canopy framework. To recover, the rudders were simply centralised, and the back pressure of the stick released to slightly forward of neutral. Here lies the problem; this technique would not work in a more conventional aircraft. The de Havilland Chipmunk, for example, required full opposite rudder followed by full forward stick as far as the stop. Even then it would 'think about it' before the rotation stopped. I was to have this lesson reinforced with a disturbing incident later in my career.

Steady progress towards my licence was dampened somewhat, when on 17 May 1966, a fellow student, Jeffery Symonds, was killed. The aircraft was found inverted with the wing detached in a paddock outside the township of Pinnaroo. Close inspection showed that it had hit the ground hard with a high vertical rate of descent with little forward speed. Investigators quickly determined the accident was caused by stalling too close to the ground during force landing practice. For its weight of 1650 lbs, the Victa Airtourer 100 was underpowered. The short stubby wings, with a span of only 26 feet, gave the aircraft a relatively high wing loading and a low power-to-weight ratio. The flaps which created both lift and drag were controlled by a spring-loaded lever mounted on both side walls of the cockpit. Selection consisted of four stages with the lever clicking into its respective slot. A combination of slow speed and the fourth stage of flap resulted in higher-than-normal sink rates for this category of aircraft. The outcome of this accident was that the fourth stage was blanked off, reducing the amount of flap to three stages only. The accident had a profound effect on me, and I took my training perhaps a little more seriously.

I finally came up for my Private Pilot flight test, and the examiner was Graham Dunn. Graham was a very reserved, almost shy man and I immediately felt relaxed and performed a safe, if nothing startling demonstration. One area where a little luck always helps was forced landings. The instructor simulates an engine failure by retarding the throttle, the student then selects a suitable area and simulates a landing without touching down. The school's rule was to overshoot at 50 feet. The hard part was positioning the aircraft 'over the fence' into wind at 50 feet without any assistance from the engine. The manoeuvre required fine judgment, considering the wind strength, and correctly assessing the sink rate and projected track over the ground. To add to the difficulty, one had to troubleshoot via a memorised checklist.

Graham, unusually, selected the paddock himself and said, "Get me in there, that dark green one with the windmill." He then closed the throttle. With part judgment and part luck, I crossed the fence exactly at 50 feet, into the wind and perfectly positioned for a landing. During the overshoot Graham looked down and back towards the retreating ground and I detected a wry grin in the corner of his mouth. He turned towards me and was indeed laughing. "Cabbages," he said, "you would have gone bum over apex if you landed there. Next time, you can pick the field!" He then reached over, shook my hand, and said, "I've seen enough, take me home." A little premature, I thought, as I still had the final landing to complete. I managed not to make a hash of it, and I was now a Private Pilot at the age of 17. Not having the money to buy a car, I would have to wait another five years before I gained a driving licence!

The licence was restricted, and to remove the restriction I needed a minimum of 20 hours of navigation training. The cost of the navigation training exercises was such that I could only complete one a month at best. The school felt this was inadequate and not practical for continuity of training.

Worse, at my high school, the results of a simulated Leaving Examination in mathematics were so poor I was summoned to appear before the headmaster. My score was an eye-watering thirty per cent. In no short order, I was told to lift my game and a report was posted to my parents. The upshot of this sad situation was that I was promptly grounded. I did apply myself and passed the end of year examinations – the only good pass was English, the rest mediocre. I immediately applied to join the Air Force as a pilot. I was shattered to be rejected outright on the first day of testing, after a poor result in maths during aptitude tests. My world seemed to be coming apart. Everywhere I turned, I seemed to be faced with insurmountable barriers.

While reading the paper one day, I saw an advertisement for a cadetship with a full-time school at Cessnock, New South Wales. I applied, was interviewed, and passed a basic selection examination and was offered a position. The only small print was the applicant had to pay up-front the full cost of the course. My parents, despite being close to retirement, took out a second mortgage on the family home and loaned me the money. I was deeply moved by this and vowed to do well.

I flew to Sydney and travelled by train to the Hunter Valley where the school was located, outside the town of Cessnock. A single sealed runway ran alongside a vineyard on one side, the school buildings were positioned on the other. Two large dormitory blocks provided the accommodation and two smaller buildings, the classrooms. There was another building for the Operations room for flight planning purposes. A large hanger and fuel pump complex completed the layout. The concept of self–funded cadetships was new to Australia, and my course was only the third batch to go through. One of the cadets on my course was Brian McCarthy who in later years would gain notoriety as the leader of the 1989 pilots' dispute. I never really saw eye to eye with Brian, finding him aloof and superior in his manner. This would have a profound effect on my decision during future events.

For reasons I have forgotten, there was some problem with the accommodation for our course and we were temporarily billeted in a disused church within the town of Cessnock. My bed was on the elevated step of what used to be the Altar. Divine intervention was slow in coming and I found the pace of the course very demanding.

Once again it was the academic side that slowed me down, but not Navigation, a subject many students found difficult. My problem was the subject Engines, Instruments and Systems. Past papers were available, and the multi-choice format proved quite elusive in gaining the correct answers. With five choices there was always one obvious wrong answer, one wrong after some thought, but at least two that seemed correct! The instructors constantly exclaimed, "Just pick the answer that is most correct," but to me this seemed a matter of opinion! The flying progressed well; I completed the navigation exercises for my Private Licence and began the Commercial syllabus which included night circuits.

I had been flying Cessnas up to this stage, both the C-150 and C-172 models. For night circuits I converted to the Piper Cherokee or PA-28. In those days, the experts decided that red instrument lighting was the way to go and the instrument panel gave off a ghostly red glow. It was during my second hour of night circuits that I looked back at the airfield and the glow reflecting in the windshield seemed brighter than normal. After a second look, I realised the hangar below was on fire. I pointed this out to Ted Banstead, my instructor, who immediately took over and we quickly landed and taxied up to the hangar. Thick smoke was noticeably pouring out of the gaps in the hanger doors.

With Ted raising the alarm and the rest of the school's occupants asleep, I ran to open the hangar doors. With the assistance of several recently arrived pyjama-clad helpers, we succeeded in opening both doors. The first aircraft, at the front, was a Cessna 188 Agwagon belonging to the local crop-duster. I climbed up onto the wing to gain access to the cockpit. While the Agwagon was a low-wing aircraft, it was unusual in that it was braced with a strut that extended mid-wing to the fuselage. Grabbing this strut, I was horrified to find it too hot to touch. Only then, did I notice the whole ceiling of the hangar was on fire and was aware of the tremendous heat in the air. Entering the cockpit, I released the brakes and with willing hands on the wings we successfully pushed the aircraft outside onto the apron. Returning to rescue the next aircraft, a Twin Comanche, we were stopped dead in our tracks by a loud hollow and very deep-sounding thump as a petrol tank in a near-by Cessna exploded.

Ted, quite correctly, ordered all and sundry to evacuate the area and we ran well clear of the burning hangar. My first refuge was none other than the nearby fuel bowsers, which, on second thought, did not seem such a good idea. I beat a hasty retreat to the grass opposite the accommodation block. We then all huddled around, watching in fascination as the hangar burnt to the ground, gas bottles exploding and the company dog barking its head off. The Fire Brigade finally arrived and with much shouting and arm waving, hoses were run out, but it was all over by now, the smoke already changing colour from black to a whitish grey.

As first person into the hangar, I was interviewed at length by the police. To my surprise, they seemed determined to charge me with some sort of offence but seemed a little unsure of what exactly. After they realised it was burning before I arrived, they changed tack but hinted we were reckless in trying to save the aircraft. I never met the owner of the Agwagon, but it appeared that he was miffed we rescued his aircraft because his insurer would have replaced it with a new one. As it was, he was reunited with his old plane complete with a paint-scorched rudder.

The fire was caused by an electrical fault; how they established that I will never know. All that was left was twisted steel beams and ashes. The complete destruction of the aircraft meant the aluminium melted into tiny balls, leaving a virtual outline of the aircraft on the hangar floor. Apart from the engines, the only other recognisable items were the seat springs still sitting neatly in their respective positions.

I passed all the Commercial examinations except for the troublesome Engines, Instruments and Systems but more bad news was to come. I was called into the office where the manager of the school explained that the costing for my course had been misquoted; no allowance for the Private Pilot navigation exercises had been included. Apparently, my quote was based on a full Private Licence and more money was required to complete the Commercial

Navigation component. This was impossible; my parents had been paying both their mortgage and my loan re-payments and could no longer do both. It was time to find a job. I left the school with the offer to return when I could pay the balance. I was now jobless with a large debt, quite a depressing state of affairs. To add insult to injury, I received a 'Dear John' letter from my girlfriend.

My parents, as always, were supportive and my father suggested I re-visit the Air Force, maybe join in the ranks, improve my education and transfer to aircrew later. Despite my obsession to begin flying as soon as possible, I have always been a realist and felt bad about exposing my parents to debt. Faced with National Service and the possibility of going into the Army and Vietnam, the Air Force suddenly looked far more attractive.

The Air Force was only too pleased to process me, and I was offered entrance via the School of Radio for training in telecommunications based at Laverton in Victoria. I accepted, and basic recruit training was held at Edinburgh in South Australia. Due to my Air Training Corps background, I passed this initial phase with no difficulty, and leaner and fitter I reported to Laverton ten weeks later. After nine months of extensive training, I was selected for Cryptographic Training which required a Top-Secret Clearance. Unknown to me at the time, ASIO conducted checks on my background which included approaching a family friend, Squadron Leader Denis Webb RAF (Ret). He was approached by a character, straight out of a spy novel, complete with raincoat and dark sunglasses. My past history was comprehensively checked, including social contacts and hobbies.

Upon completing the course, I began to work in the secure de-coding room in the communications centre located at Frognall, a Melbourne suburb. I enjoyed this work, finding it interesting and more importantly, with night shift, it gave me the opportunity to join the RAAF Flying Club at the nearby base of Point Cook. Here I could continue my flying studies. I finally passed the Engines,

Instruments and Systems examination and with a steady income, I managed not only to meet my debt obligations but also to save enough to complete my Commercial navigation exercises. Squadron Leader Kevin Duffy, an Engineering Officer and pilot, oversaw the Club and again, I found someone supportive. Completing my remaining Navigational exercises, I finally passed my Commercial Licence test at Moorabbin Airport. At last, I was on my way forward; it was a great psychological victory.

The Air Force Club was supplied with aircraft from Peninsula Air Services of Moorabbin and operated on a civilian Air Operations Certificate. Peninsula Air Services was owned and operated by a colourful character, Dr Bill Surh, a Frankston dentist. Bill was a total aviation enthusiast, a rebel to the establishment and had a delightful sense of humour. Despite my lowly status, not to mention the age difference, he accepted me as a fellow 'wingnut', as he called us, and went out of his way to encourage my progress. Bill offered me a part-time job flying the Radio 3DB traffic patrol over Melbourne city. The task was to simply fly with a Radio Announcer in the back and seek out any traffic snarls during peak period. Working at night with the RAAF suited me as I could grab some sleep on the completion of my shift, fly in the morning and sleep again in the afternoon.

On the weekends the 3DB station operated a Shark Patrol around the bayside beaches and I rotated between both tasks. If a shark was sighted, we dropped into a low, tight orbit and sounded an air horn. The announcer in the back would then broadcast a dramatic description of events. Philip was another budding pilot who flew the 3DB flights – he also had a regular job with the local bank.

One weekend, after spotting a large group of sharks off Mud Island, Phil wrapped the aircraft into a steep turn approaching the vertical. The aircraft stalled and then cart-wheeled into the water. Despite having a closer inspection of the sharks than intended, both occupants miraculously survived. More ominously, Philip was nicknamed 'Phil the Dill' and his reputation was ruined. I felt terribly sorry for him and he faded into obscurity. I never forgot the lesson of 'reputation.' In aviation you are remembered by your mistakes, not your achievements.

One day, the RAAF News printed an article about the 3DB operation, which was called Snoopy by the local press. 'A RAAF airman is the pilot', screamed the title, giving out my name and rank. Not unnaturally, my boss, Squadron Leader Cowburn, called me into his office and wanted to know, "What the hell is going on?" Instead of delivering a dressing down, he was most sympathetic and wanted to know why I had not applied for aircrew; he was ex-aircrew himself. After I explained my tales of rejection, he said he would back me to the hilt to fly as a civilian and get out of the Air Force. "No Air Force Officer worth a damn would stop a man from flying!" he told me.

Bill Surh wrote a letter confirming an offer of full-time employment and I applied under Air Force Regulation 118 (On Request) to leave. Normally a discharge under this section of Air Force Regulations was extremely rare and difficult to obtain, but I gained support in high places and the application was approved. It was with some sadness I resigned from the RAAF. The upside – I was now a professional pilot, albeit on minimum wages, heavily in debt and completely homeless, but I had finally made it!

3
CHARTER PILOT
1972–1977

*Life is not measured by the breaths you take
but the moments that take your breath away.*

Mark Twain

Bill Surh very kindly allowed me to complete an Instructor Rating and to take it out in wages; the only problem was that my cash flow was now the bare minimum to survive. I had no car, not having the time or money to obtain a driving licence, used book staples to repair my shoes and lived on a diet of baked beans on toast. It was in this sorry state I met my first wife who was working for the Civil Aviation Authority as a receptionist.

I enjoyed my new job, meeting people from all walks of life and was sent over to Point Cook to be a civilian instructor at the Air Force Club. Here under the watchful eyes of my old mentor, Squadron Leader Duffy, I steadily built up experience and learnt the trade.

One day he wanted to test my ability to teach spinning in De Havilland Chipmunks and climbed into the back seat while I was in the front. We took off and climbed to 6,000 feet over the airfield and entered a spin to the left. Unfortunately, KD as we called him, at more than twice my weight that far back, shifted the aircraft's centre of gravity. The Chipmunk immediately went into a flat spin with the nose 'hunting' through the horizon. Flat spins are dangerous because with a high nose attitude the wings blank off the airflow over the tail. The propeller stopped and here we were, totally stable, despite all attempts to recover, slowly spinning towards the ground.

Strangely, I felt no panic, more a feeling of sadness that after all this effort, I was just going to be a hole in the ground! To KD's credit, he took over and with his engineering background, understood the problem and began to rock the flaps up and down. With this action, together with some heat turbulence, we were finally able to force the nose down and affect a recovery. It gave us both a nasty fright.

This was not the only incident with the Chipmunk; several pilots had been killed while spinning. The aircraft were subsequently modified with spin strakes, streamlined fairings where the tailplane joined the fuselage. This had the effect of keeping the tail 'alive' by providing a smooth flow over the tailplane at high-nose attitudes.

I was starting to understand aviation; while not dangerous in isolation, it required one to keep an eye on the ball and could be very unforgiving. Sadly, this revelation was further emphasised when Jim O'Connell was killed flying his recently restored De Havilland Dragon, a beautiful twin-engine biplane dating back to the thirties. Jim was an engineer for Forrester Stephens based at Essendon and a keen private pilot. I watched him lovingly restore this aircraft in one of Point Cook's vacant hangers. I greatly enjoyed hangar talk with him, crawling over the aeroplane and having a cold beer afterwards. Finally completing the restoration, Jim took off into a gusting northerly wind, lost an engine and tried to turn back to the field. The aircraft stalled at low level and struck the ground bursting into flames. All that remained was a black patch on the grass with a few twisted pieces of airframe.

I enjoyed instructing, flying a wide variety of aircraft including Chipmunks, Airtourers, various Cessnas and Pipers and some odd balls like the Fletcher Fu24 and a Republic Sea Bee. The Fletcher was an agricultural aircraft. Bill had two cargo conversions for transporting muttonbirds from the Bass Strait Islands. I only flew the aircraft locally, not having the experience to operate among the short and demanding strips on the islands. I needed more charter experience to move up the ladder and with Bill's blessing, I applied to join Lanham's Air Charter of Mt Isa. The job was passenger and freight runs to the large cattle stations in North West Queensland. The runs extended north to the Gulf of Carpentaria and west to the Northern Territory border. The application proved successful and with my new young wife, we set off for another life.

One amusing incident during the journey was the transportation of our pet parrot. My wife insisted it travel with us. After we hired a pet pack from the airline, it quickly became obvious the bird was in some distress. I came up with the idea of slipping some brandy into its drinking water, thinking this would calm the thing down. On arrival at Mt Isa, it appeared I exceeded the sensible dosage, as the bird was quite drunk, hanging upside down in its cage like a bat and shrieking a continuous stream of very garbled "hello Pollys". This was not the elegant arrival I had planned when I met the owner, John Lanham, in the airport terminal.

Lanham Air charter was a family business. Cliff Lanham, the family head, ran a joyride and charter company on the Queensland Gold Coast. John, one of three sons, operated the Mt Isa charter side along with his wife Heather. Cliff Lanham was a man of strong religious beliefs and it was said the 'good boys' were selected for the Gold Coast and the 'bad boys' sent to the desert. I never found out if this was true or not but I never felt that Mt Isa was the short end of the stick. On the contrary, I had flown the joy-flight operation for a week and that was enough. Mt Isa was hard charter, and this was more to my liking. The fleet consisted of mainly single-engine

Cessnas and two single-engine Beechcraft, one B33 Debonair and one V35 Bonanza. The Cessna's were 206, 207 and 210 models. I was given only a day to settle into the accommodation and complete administration duties and was expected to fly the next day.

It was then I discovered I was replacing a pilot who had just been killed. The industry grapevine was normally quicker than Telecom, but for some reason I had not heard of the accident. During a night take-off from Boulia, south of Mt Isa, the pilot had become spatially disorientated and had dived at high speed into the ground. Night flying in remote areas could be deadly with few lights for visual orientation, and without an instrument rating a pilot could lose control very quickly. Due to limitations of the human ear and no visual horizon, false sensations could be experienced; in the flying world we call this 'the leans'.

I flew with John the next day, doing one session of circuits followed by a short station run to one homestead. John appeared happy with my basic handling and the next day I was rostered on my first trip flying a Cessna 207. I had some previous experience on the Cessna 206, but never at maximum take-off weight and while the 207 looked basically similar it was a different animal. Cessna stretched the fuselage by some four feet with extensions both forward and aft, behind the wing. With the same 300hp Lycoming engine, the 207 weighed 200 lbs more than the 206 and could carry seven people. Later versions could carry a total of eight people with a reduction in take-off fuel. The loaded aircraft sat tail low with its powerful snout reducing forward visibility and accelerated much more slowly than I had previously experienced.

On my first take-off at maximum weight, with the propeller tips snarling, I staggered into the hot humid air. With the aircraft's shadow racing across the rock-strewn scrub, I could barely manage 300 feet per minute rate of climb. The heat was unbearable, even the control column showed signs of corrosion from human sweat. The 'salt' had pitted the black paint around the natural hand-grip.

The sun reflected off hundreds of tiny scratch marks on the windshield and looking out along the underneath of the wing, slashes of green primer showed through the worn paint. No doubt about it, this was a working man's aeroplane!

Reaching 4,000 feet, the aircraft showed a distinct reluctance to climb any further and I adjusted the mixture and cowl flaps and trimmed for cruise. After an hour, my first stop, Iffley Station came into view. Navigation was proving easier than I thought. With so few features, anything of note stuck out for miles. The dried-out riverbeds all had tree growth, highlighting the river's direction and map reading was proving quite straightforward.

As I banked over the homestead, the station name appeared in large black letters on the roof, further confirming all was well. I set myself up to fly a standard square circuit at 1,000 feet and landed with a light bounce on the uneven strip, trailing a great cloud of red dust. Pulling up alongside a simple shelter that served as a terminal, I shut the engine down and opened the door.

A rough-looking character introduced himself as the Station Manager, swatting off hundreds of flies as he did so. "Thought you were going to fly past," he said with a hint of sarcasm. "Haven't seen anybody fly that wide an approach before. Lucky, we heard you," he continued, "normally they buzz the station and just split-arse onto the runway." I smiled, but secretly took note. "You are new," he said with a whistle – he was looking down at my shoes. The Air Force had taught me how to polish shoes to a mirror shine and it was with these I was standing in the red dust. "Desert boots, mate," was all he said, as he began to unload the mail.

With the load transferred to the back of the Land Rover, I bade farewell and climbed back aboard the aircraft. When I attempted to start the engine, it spluttered once but failed to keep running. The Station Manager yelled through the open window, "Vapour lock, mate, just give it more fuel." The Cessna high/low fuel pump provided the extra fuel and the engine roared into life. With a

Cheshire Cat grin, he gave me a half wave and turned towards his vehicle.

My 'new boy' status suitably noted, I took off for Escott Station, the next destination. Escott was further north, just inland from the Gulf and surrounded by tall trees. The strip was simply a slash in the tree line with the station alongside. I flew over low and tight as I checked the windsock and positioned myself for a close circuit. I could not do much about the desert boots, but I could show them my flying! Once below the tree line, I hit rolling turbulence and found myself over-controlling with the wings rocking left and right like a drunk. I hit the ground with a firm thud and bounced back into the air for a second untidy arrival. Once I shut down the engine, the welcoming party all had that same stupid grin on their faces and I now felt much deflated. No comments were made until I climbed back into the aircraft. "Normanton is over there, mate," said a stockman with an exaggerated wave of his arm.

I took off empty for the short trip to Normanton where I would take on fuel and a load of prawns for the trip home. The landing proved straightforward with the refrigerated van waiting patiently on the apron. Again, nothing much was said as I helped load the plastic bins through the aircraft's double doors. Airborne again, I had difficulty raising Mount Isa on the HF radio, finally passing my departure details after some delay. I was now feeling the heat and felt exhausted. I still had a freight run to Gunpowder, a mine just north of Mount Isa, on return.

This charter pilot business was hard work and I made a mental note to carry more water. There seemed so much to learn, and it was remarkably different from Instructing down south. The midday sun produced pockets of violent turbulence and it was with some relief I sighted the red and white chimneys of the Mount Isa mine. Due to the sandy terrain, the radio navigation aid, the NDB (Non-Directional Beacon) had a limited range, especially for low flying light aircraft. On a clear day one would spot the chimneys with their red and white stripes long before the Morse-code ident of the NDB would come through the headphones. Thus, the chimneys were referred to by the charter pilots as the 'smoking NDB'. Decades later, flying high over Mt Isa in a 747 I would often sight the 'smoking NDB' and this would always result in an inward chuckle – it always looked the same.

So began my charter career. I bought a pair of desert boots, a 'cool' pair of sunglasses and a large water bottle. I flew tight circuits with panache, started boiling engines on first attempt and turned towards the next destination as soon as I was airborne. The only thing I did not know was how inexperienced I was and how dangerous this period in a young pilot's career could be.

After a month I started to get into a routine and became accepted by the customers, losing my 'sprog' status but still found the length of duty exhausting. Some days stretched to 8 hours of stick (flying) and 14 of duty. While duty limits were limited by regulation, in those days, enforcement was lax. I have never blamed John Lanham for this, indeed even today we remain in contact and good friends.

The station owners depended on us as their sole contact with the outside world. The very nature of the beast required great flexibility on our part to get the job done. A machine part would need replacing when it failed and during the wet season with the roads closed, we were the only source of transport. We worked hard to get the task complete, often in bad weather which could vary from thunderstorms to blowing dust. We often completed favours for the station owners, checking fence-lines on the way home or seeing if a certain bore was working. The bores were wind-driven by large windmill blades that could be easily checked by flying low alongside them. Neighbours could be fifty miles apart but exchanging spare parts or even a frying pan was common.

In my second month, I received the good news that a new pilot, John Grace, was joining the company. I knew John from my instructing days; he was, at the time, instructing out of Berwick, just south of Moorabbin. I often landed there with a student on the pretext of landing at an unfamiliar airport, but primarily to gain a glimpse of Eve Turner, a stunning blonde Instructor who wore 'hot pants', fashionable at the time. John was highly amused by this and we became good friends.

On John's arrival, I was tasked with familiarising him on the Cessna 210, a type he had not flown, and we had a very pleasant reunion. Shortly after this time, Northwest Queensland entered the wet season with a vengeance, the season producing the worst floods on record. One by one, the station strips became unusable due to 'soft wet surface' as described by the NOTAMs (Notice to Airmen). The only way to keep the stations supplied with the essentials, especially food, was to air drop them. We removed the Cessna's rear doors and flew with a 'kicker' – a staff member solely responsible for throwing the supplies out on the pilot's command. This demanded low and slow flying and a level of accuracy that was not as easy to obtain as it might seem.

The biggest problem was minimising the damage to the goods. Oddly enough, one of the hardest items to drop was bread. On my first attempt over Smoky Creek Station, I was surprised during the pull-up to see individual slices of bread flying through the treetops, like shrapnel from a bomb burst. I promised the station manager over the radio that I would return for another attempt. This time we packed the bread into sugar bags, tied the tops down with wire and roared back into the air. Once over the station I flew down to 50 feet just off the stall and gave the order to release, only to see bread once more going in all directions.

We finally used a version of a system invented by a pilot in Victoria where the flaps of a cardboard box are used as helicopter blades, folded outside and out, causing the box to spin and reducing its rate of descent. After a while, I became particularly good at this delivery system, once placing a box of supplies onto a homestead's veranda. (The fact that I was aiming for the front lawn would spoil a good story).

Inevitably we had incidents with this risky type of flying and once nearly lost John Grace. His escape can only be described as miraculous. Over McAllister Station just south of the Gulf (Gulf of Carpentaria), John had just completed a drop and failed to see the station HF radio aerial. This he hit with the right wing, the aerial tearing a line under the wing skin and hitting the leading edge of the right aileron, which deflected up in the turn with the leading-edge protruding just below the wing surface. The aileron was ripped out, except for a small area around the hinge attachment point and fluttered gently to the ground to join the supplies. John instinctively applied full opposite rudder and what remained of the ailerons, but even then, had trouble stopping the aircraft's tendency to roll over inverted. Flying along in this perilous crab-like fashion, John managed to divert to nearby Normanton and make a safe landing. It was truly an amazing demonstration of flying skill and we laughed about it for years. It did, however, have a sobering effect on him and John knew that Lady Luck was with him that day; another inch lower and he would have lost a wing.

As for myself, I once had a mail bag wrap around the left elevator, all attempts to get it to fall off failing. The controls were restricted but not critically and I elected to land with the flaps retracted so as not to aggravate the situation further. All the Cessna 200 series had powerful flaps with a large pitching moment when lowered; I considered it unwise to experiment. On landing, only a handful of letters remained in the bag, the rest were scattered over the countryside.

A few weeks later I had another unusual incident while flying just south of Boulia, a tiny outpost south of Mt Isa. Lying neatly on the ground was a line of white stones spelling out 'SOS APPENDIX.' Beside the stones were a small outstation, a dirt road and two people surrounded by flood water waving madly at the aircraft.

I tried to contact Mt Isa on the HF radio but could only raise Townsville who kept asking my intentions. I decided that I could land on the road and rescue both occupants, but I had to do it immediately due to the aircraft's fuel state. The operator in Townsville kept saying, "Negative, standby," and then asked if I was declaring a Mercy Flight. Once declared, this allowed some relaxation of certain rules, subject to the pilot in command's judgement. I declared that this was indeed my intention and again he said, "Standby for approval." I did not have the fuel for further mind-numbing procrastination and set the aircraft up for a landing on the narrow dirt track.

There was only just enough room for the main wheels on the two-wheel tracks, as the centre was grass. On lowering the nose wheel, the centre section proved extremely rough with the instrument panel almost shaking itself apart. I shut down and was met by a very distraught stockman who said his mate was in an unbelievably bad way with what he suspected was appendicitis. It was obvious that I would be unable to take off with the centre of this track in its present state; it was one thing to lower the nose at low speed during landing but it was entirely another, taking off with the load initially on the nose wheel. I made contact again with Townsville asking for medical assistance via an air drop from Mt Isa. Thinking I was still in the air, all I received was permission to land. It took some time to convince him I was way ahead of his mental picture and he said help was on the way.

An hour later John Lanham himself appeared overhead in a twin-engine Beechcraft Baron, complete with a doctor – an incredibly quick response. Medicine was air dropped and the doctor over the radio gave me an instant lesson in how to administer an injection. This was all completed, and the patient made comfortable in a nearby vehicle. A further two hours passed and a RAAF Iroquois helicopter, with its main rotor blades loudly slapping the air, landed in a cloud of flying debris and water spray and quickly loaded the patient. The rotor noise made conversation difficult, and with minimal fuss it took off and promptly disappeared. The remaining stockman and I seemed to have been left out of the argument!

After I explained the problem for our take-off, my companion, in true bush style, quickly produced two long-handled shovels and we set about removing a couple of hundred feet of this centre grass. We completed this in three hours which completely exhausted both of us. Neither of us had eaten all day but luckily, we had ample water supplies. I could not afford to risk remaining battery power prior to engine start in contacting anybody and finally we were ready to attempt a take-off. Using full back-stick and lowering the flaps on the run we were successful, but once airborne I had doubts about having enough fuel to reach Mt Isa.

I managed to contact Mount Isa on HF (High Frequency) and spoke with John Lanham who instructed me to land at Boulia. The strip was still available despite the floods. On the ground there, I finally got to speak to John on the phone and was somewhat dismayed to learn there was no fuel available. To cut a long story short, we managed to acquire some automotive fuel from the local Shell dealer and after a long conversation with the engineers we were allowed to mix just enough with the aircraft fuel to get home. This we did, and apart from running a little hotter, the engine showed no distress at all. The aircraft then had all the remaining fuel completely drained and seeing this was a blend, we received permission to use it in the company car. The disappointing outcome of this arrangement was that the Morris Minor, complete with an 'indestructible side-valve engine', promptly blew itself up. However, the patient made a full recovery, albeit without his appendix.

It was sometime later that I also had a close call and this forced my hand in leaving Lanham's and obtaining an Instrument Rating. I was rostered to fly the 207 to transport a generator to Rockhampton via Longreach for repair. The generator filled the cabin to the roof and the aircraft was at maximum weight. Once airborne, I flew via Cloncurry and then tracked towards Winton. As I approached Winton, the cloud became progressively thicker and lower and by the time I picked up the railway line linking Winton to Longreach I was 'scud running'. This is the term pilots use to describe sitting just below an extremely low cloud base and the ground. I should have turned back but was now tantalisingly close and while forward visibility was virtually zero, I had my railway line, and I knew this would lead me to the airport. I was now down below 200 feet, totally insane in retrospect, but young pilots in their twenties are well known for moments of insanity.

Suddenly out of the mist, I spotted two red lights racing towards me. "Bloody hell, it's somebody else coming the opposite way doing the same thing!" I pulled up hard and over into a right-climbing turn, quickly entering cloud as I did so. It was now critical to ignore all outside sensations and concentrate just on the flight instruments. After what seemed like a period of time standing still, I finally popped out into brilliant sunshine on top of a very flat layer of stratus cloud. With a dry mouth and thumping heart, I continued 'on top' and found Longreach in a large hole for an uneventful landing.

I spent the night in the local motel, but had a very restless sleep, still rattled by the day's events. The return flight proved to be two beautiful clear days without a cloud in the sky. Arriving back at Longreach, I had another restless night still thinking about my previous visit.

The following morning, I hurried down to the airport for the empty ferry flight back home. Once airborne, I decided to backtrack via the railway line as something about those lights was bothering me, particularly the fact they were both red, and not red and green as per normal aircraft lights. Sure enough, my worst fears were realised – in the position of my break-off was the largest microwave tower I had ever seen, with the red lights obviously attached to the microwave discs. It was something else that really made the hair on my neck stand up – from the top of the tower, giant stay wires radiated out and down to the ground. I could not see how I could have flown so close to it without hitting those wires, especially in its position relative to the railway line. It just did not seem possible. I flew quietly home very subdued, but my mind was made up – it was time to do an instrument rating. John was disappointed in my resignation and tried to talk me into staying but I was convinced it was time to move on.

On arriving back in Melbourne, I managed to secure a job with Moorabbin Aviation Academy as an instructor and during my spare time commenced the expensive instrument rating. I had trouble settling back into disciplined flying, not realising how the rough and tumble of charter work had affected my accuracy in the more precise area of Instrument Flying. With some frustration, I again had trouble financing the training and had to take a break to consolidate. I was simply not prepared to borrow money again and tried to pay for the sessions on the run.

Finally, I finished the rating with John Correll, flying a Twin Comanche, VH-CON or Oscar Nuts as nicknamed by the dozens of students who cut their teeth on this venerable machine. John Lindsay was the Departmental Examiner doing my check-out. John was a charming man, very fair but at the same time demanded a good standard and totally dedicated to the industry. Over the years I was checked by him on numerous occasions and always felt comfortable with his laidback style. During a test he would often sit quietly reading a magazine or stare out the window at the ground below, but he never missed a thing. How he knew what you had just tried to cover up while appearing not to be looking remained a mystery. The secret was just to admit it – "I know, I saw that," he would say.

Just after I completed the instrument rating, I quickly discovered that all the operators wanted 500 hours of multi-engine engine experience (twin-time) before they would look at you. I could not see how anybody could get 500 hours twin-time unless they first gave you a job! I was offered a job with Civil Flying School and took it immediately as they operated several twin-engine aircraft. However, it was back to basic instructing again which I enjoyed, but after my wild charter days, doing circuits in a Beechcraft Musketeer with a student was like watching paint dry.

There were the occasional charters – I remember one as my first commercial charter under Instrument Flight Rules. The job was to fly to Goondiwindi in Queensland and retrieve the body of a young girl who had been accidentally shot on her honeymoon by her new husband. I never did discover the official circumstances of this tragedy, but the story went that he was helping her under a wire fence with a loaded gun in his other hand and it snagged on the barbed wire and discharged, killing her instantly. I could not imagine a more tragic set of circumstances and it was with some trepidation that I took off and headed to Queensland.

I was flying a single-engine Beechcraft A36 Bonanza and arrived in Goondiwindi in the late afternoon. Despite dreading being confronted by grieving relatives, I was surprised to be met by only a funeral director and his driver. With the poor girl safely aboard, I took off into the fading light and headed back to Moorabbin. Flying alone at night with a dead body behind me was not quite what I expected for my first use of my new instrument rating.

On landing, the Chief Pilot found my discarded flight plan and gave me a verbal rocket for annotating the Persons on Board as 'one.' His quite valid point was that if I had gone down and been thrown clear of the wreck, those who found one body already on board would not have looked for another. I thought of pointing out to him that the deceased was female, and not only that, but with a gunshot wound and inside a body-bag. I decided to let him have his 'regulatory moment' and said nothing.

These breaks in the monotony were few. Just when all seemed lost, one of the local private pilots who hired aircraft from the company quietly informed me that he was going to buy a Cessna 310. Not having an instrument rating, he asked me if I would like to fly it for his company. A high-performance twin for its day, this was exactly the opportunity I needed. When I told the Chief Pilot, he tried to talk me into making instructing a career. There was some resentment in those days to young instructors 'hour building' and then leaving for a better paid job.

Hog Industries was a small company in the electronic assembly business taking advantage of the Victorian Government's generous tax rebates for the De-Centralisation program. This was designed to encourage business to move away from the cities and into the countryside. The company had a factory installed in a disused hangar at Bairnsdale airport. My task was to fly company staff both to the factory and onto Sydney, the home of one of the directors. My old boss Bill Surh endorsed me on his elderly C-310B model which was not a true representation of the newer Q model. This was pointed out to me by one of the senior instructors at Civil Flying School and I agreed to some training with an instructor (dual time) on the company aircraft as well.

I enjoyed the work, the aircraft was nice to fly, fast and manoeuvrable, it would indicate 190 knots at sea level and was considered a bit of a hot-rod. I began to fly into 'real weather' and gained valuable experience doing Non-Directional Beacon let-downs to land at Bairnsdale. The Non-Directional Beacon was a Very High Frequency navigational aid. A simple compass-dialled instrument superimposed with a pointer in the cockpit would simply point to the tuned station. It was an acquired skill to maintain an accurate track, inbound or outbound to the station allowing for drift caused by the wind. Once the aircraft is positioned over the top of the transmitter it was possible to fly a published procedure for a descent to below the cloud base. Once established visually with the ground, the aircraft could be then manoeuvred for a landing. A minimum safe altitude was published based on local conditions and obstacles. Due to the design of the approach regarding terrain, the Non-Directional Bearing invariably had the final inbound track away from runway alignment. This resulted in a low-level circling manoeuvre.

During training for the instrument rating this was the navigational aid that most pilots found difficult to grasp. Once mastered, it was extremely satisfying to fly accurately and pop out of cloud exactly as per the chart. The Non-Directional Beacon is now being replaced by more sophisticated navigation procedures using satellite aids such as GPS and only a few remain. In the US they have disappeared entirely.

I quickly discovered ice in the winter months, and found the ice coming off the propellers and hitting the fuselage was disturbing, and I was careful not to push it. Sadly, the job was not to last, as 'unplanned maintenance' caused the company accountant sleepless nights. In one week alone, the aircraft chewed up two expensive suction pumps. These pumps provided vital instrument data and were notoriously unreliable, partly because they were designed with a nylon shaft that would shear under load. When the inevitable came, I had just over 300 hours on the machine but nevertheless, I was unemployed again.

Bill Surh kept my spirits up by endorsing me on the Cessna 337, the Beechcraft Baron and the Cessna 401. The 337 was an odd twin-engine machine having centre line thrust with one engine on the nose and one in the tail. The aircraft was owned by a Dr Ward, a friend of Bill's and registered VH-DND. This was quickly nicknamed Death 'n' Disaster and I flew it only for a few hours. It was very noisy, partly because the rear propeller was slashing away at air already disturbed by the wings. A military version called a Cessna O-2 proved successful during the Vietnam War acting as a Forward Air Controller. The job of an FAC was to hunt down targets and then direct strike aircraft to attack them. How you could sneak up on anybody with the noise of a demented chainsaw remains a mystery.

Bill suggested I apply to Australian Air Charterers, considered the premium operator on the field. AAC was owned by Industrial Hardware, a family business owned by Bill Dart or Darty as he was known. The company operated a fleet of twin-engine aircraft on government contracts, including the Premier's Contract, flying state and federal ministers about. They also serviced the lighthouse on Gabo Island and conducted an air sampling contract for the State Electricity Commission. On top of this impressive list, the company flew newspapers to Canberra on a nightly basis and conducted crew changes for the oil industry. The fleet consisted of Piper Navajos, Chieftains, Aztecs, an executive pressurised Cessna 414 and a Twin Comanche.

The Manager and Chief Pilot was Graeme Lowe, ably assisted in the office by his wife Betty. Because I could not meet the 500-hour requirement on twins, I did not fancy my chances but thought it worth a try. True to form, Graeme was friendly but rejected me based on my lack of experience. As I left rather dejectedly, Betty, as I was to find out later, admonished Graeme and told him to, "Give the poor bastard a go." I was called back inside and offered a job on probation, flying initially the Twin Comanche to see how I performed. I was over the moon; this was the break I so desperately needed.

The Twin Comanche was a popular twin-trainer of the time and had a reputation of being a bit of a 'pilot killer.' For a twin, the aircraft was small, weighing in at 3,725 lbs and equipped with two 160hp engines and seated up to five passengers, although it was only a four-seater with any respectable fuel load.

The problem lay in the fact it had a high Velocity Minimum Control speed. In any conventional multi-engine aeroplane, if power is lost on one side, the thrust remaining is asymmetrical. This 'unbalanced' thrust can easily be controlled by rudder and aileron, providing a healthy forward speed is maintained. The minimum speed possible in this configuration is termed Velocity Minimum Control or more commonly VMC. There is a minimum speed both on the ground and in the air, referred to as VMCG and VMCA respectively.

The Twin Comanche had a VMCA of 80 knots but also a relatively high stall speed due to the 'Laminar' design of the wing. As mentioned in an earlier chapter, a stall is a loss of lift. To explain further, the stall is an aerodynamic breakdown of airflow which occurs if the wing is at too high an angle to the relative airflow. This angle is called the Angle of Attack. Once an aerofoil reaches a critical angle of attack, the smooth airflow breaks down into a turbulent eddy and the surface loses lift or stalls.

The Twin Comanche's problem was at certain combinations of altitude and temperature, the VMCA and the stall speed could come together. This could produce a nasty loss of control which invariably led to an unrecoverable flat spin. Several Instructors demonstrating VMCA during training were killed this way. The problem was partially fixed by adding small metal strips to the leading edge of the wing to delay the onset of stall, as well as better training of instructors.

The reputation of the aircraft, unfairly, remained. One well-deserved reputation was that it was difficult to land. The aircraft was noticeably short-legged, the trailing edge of the wing was only two feet from the ground. This had the effect of trapping a cushion of air under the wings during landing making it difficult to 'sit' the aircraft down. This phenomenon is called ground effect and to make matters worse, the Twin Comanche had the same size nose wheel as the main wheels. Often while in ground effect, the nose wheel would make contact while the wings were still flying causing an unpleasant 'pigrooting' as the aircraft skipped from nose wheel to main wheels. Trying to impress a passenger with one's flying skill could often end up in a degrading episode of leaps and bounces that could deflate any ego. The Americans offered a modified nose wheel of smaller dimensions as a retrofit, the downside being less ground clearance to the propellers, and I am not aware of any Australian aircraft being fitted with this option.

Once in the air the aeroplane was a delight to fly, light on the controls and very manoeuvrable. The company aircraft was fitted with wing-tip tanks and Rayjay turbochargers, giving it good performance and an endurance of over six hours. The fuel system consisted of six tanks but only two fuel gauges which showed only the two tanks selected at the time. It was important to keep a mental picture of what fuel remained and where it was located on the aircraft. Years later, I realised what good training this was for flight management and general situation awareness but at the time I considered it a complete pain.

After only two months of flying this little monster, Graeme endorsed me on the rest of the fleet. I began to feel like one of the regulars. Graeme ran the company like an Air Force Squadron – every Friday night, all available pilots and ground engineers would join Graeme and Betty for a few beers. This resulted in a very tight and professional team, long before Human Resources were invented and other trendy team-building programmes.

The pilots at the time were a mixed group: Lindsay Ingram was an ex-schoolteacher, David Butlin a former agricultural pilot, Len Cleary was older and a father figure. Greg Smith was my age and a total aviation enthusiast, Bill Fone, profoundly serious and mature, and David Wilkinson a dashing ladies' man, looking very much what the public perceived a pilot should look like. Lyle Macintosh joined us later, tall, and dry, typical country boy. To add to this splendid group, we had casual pilots to take up the slack during busy periods. These included Keith Meggs, Bob Thorpe, Peter Benton, and Jim Miller. Keith was an ex-fighter pilot who flew with the famous 77 squadron in Korea and we became firm friends and remain so to this day. Unfortunately, Peter was to die on the newspaper run following an engine failure on take-off and Jim was to perish in a Twin-Otter crash in New Guinea after experiencing an in-flight fire.

The Piper Navajo and Chieftain were good-looking aircraft and a delight to fly, proving the adage 'If it looks right, it will fly right.' The Navajo was an eight-seat light twin and the larger Chieftain could seat up to ten. The Navajo had two 310hp engines and the Chieftain two slightly larger engines of 350hp. The Chieftain would carry 900kg of newspapers and the Navajo 800kg.

A typical newspaper flight would start at Moorabbin Airport just before midnight. After a cup of coffee, we would check in with Air Traffic on the phone, with a standard flight plan lodged. Taxiing out together, one aircraft behind the other, we would depart for Melbourne's Tullamarine Airport to pick up the papers from the Trans Australia Airlines freight shed. With the seats removed a sheet of plywood was laid on the floor and protective canvas sheets lined the cabin wall. The fuel load consisted of full main tanks and half-full outer tanks.

During the take-off from Moorabbin the aircraft would accelerate rapidly, and at take-off speed, slight back pressure on the control column would have the aircraft leaping into the air and climbing away with a deep growl from the turbochargers. After the undercarriage was raised, the power would be reduced to the climb setting, propeller pitch and mixtures adjusted, and both cowl flaps opened fully for the climb. Flaps up, fuel pumps and landing lights off and we would be already turning at 3000 feet towards the locator beacon at Essendon, known as the 'Plenty Locator.' Even after more than forty years, I can still remember the track of 358 and the frequency of the Plenty Locator as 218.

From there, we tracked to Epping and down the Instrument Landing System for runway 27 at Tullamarine. With no other traffic at that time of day, Air Traffic Control would allow us any speed we liked, and it became a source of pride to fly flat out. We were limited only by the operational restrictions, mainly the flap and undercarriage speed limits.

Once on the ground, the aircraft were parked outside the freight shed in preparation for loading. The time taken to load varied according to the weather, and during this time we would chat with the TAA staff and complete a load sheet. Airline freight sheds, especially at night, were very strange places. The workers always looked like pirates and vagabonds to me, complete with coloured beanies and scarfs. The language was invariably colourful, with forklifts and other lifting devices racing around creating an atmosphere of complete bedlam. Somehow, among this controlled mayhem, we would receive our load and be on our way.

The aircraft's performance at maximum weight was nothing like the departure out of Moorabbin, with howling turbochargers glowing white hot, visible through the engine's cowl grill as the aircraft struggled to maintain 500 feet a minute climb. More ominously, the aircraft felt unstable in pitch. The elevator felt unusually light, passing the message that the centre of gravity was at its aft limit. This is where we were most vulnerable, not only to an engine failure, but the dreaded ice as we climbed up through the cloud.

I would watch the engine instruments like a hawk to detect any early signs of a problem. We had no anti-ice protection and no weather radar, relying on our wits to keep us out of trouble. When faced with the summer thunderstorms, we would watch the lightning flashes to detect the worst areas and try to avoid them and stay below the cloud base. This would often place the aircraft in a squall line with heavy rain and turbulence and could be extremely nerve-wracking.

The HF aerial proved to be a most effective 'ice marker'. With the build-up of ice, the aerial which ran from the fin to the wing tip would lose its 'curve' in the slipstream and go dead straight – giving ample warning to check the leading edge of the wings by torchlight. Ice building up on the propellers would also be flung onto the side of the nose with a loud bang. Ice striking the aircraft like that would invariably cause the failure of the cabin/cockpit heater. The heater required an air-source for its operation and in severe icing, the inlet would freeze over and cause the heater to backfire once or twice and subsequently fail. Lindsay Ingram, ever resourceful, carried a sleeping bag with the bottom cut out and would wear it with his feet protruding out to operate the rudder pedals. I would just put up with it, not liking to restrict my feet, but the cold could be unbearable at times.

Obviously in extreme conditions we always had the option to divert. In two years of doing the paper run, I only had to divert once, dropping into Wagga to avoid a nasty thunderstorm. With me that night, flying the second aeroplane, was a new pilot on his first trip. Lindsay Ingram in a third aircraft managed to get through, but the new boy landed behind me at Wagga. After climbing out of the aircraft, I walked over to discuss our departure. I found him wide-eyed and visibly upset. "You blokes are completely barking mad," he said, and he refused to go on. He never flew with us again but went on to become a Captain with Cathay Pacific. It all seemed normal to me and I worried that I might be missing something.

Once on the ground at Canberra, we would raid the leftovers with the consent of the TAA catering section, and get quite a decent meal, especially off the first-class trays. Once the load was off, refuelling was accomplished by manually pulling a hose out from a fixed hydrant, a miserable job in winter, especially if yours was the last aircraft, because once finished, the hose had to be wound back in. The flight home with an empty aircraft was invariably straightforward but sometimes we would take a portable oxygen bottle to get above 10,000ft and avoid the worst of the weather. Trying to sleep during the day always proved to be a problem with noisy lawnmowers and all the other trappings of 'normal people' going about their business. I remember once abusing some poor girl trying to sell me a pen on a telemarketing phone call on behalf of the blind. I felt terrible afterwards, but it indicates the problem of shift workers.

Graeme was very aware of fatigue and would roster us back to daylight flying for a week on the other contracts or general charter. Gabo Island was one of my favourites, when flown by the Aztec or Navajo. The Gabo Island lighthouse was situated just off the coast on the Victorian and New South Wales border with a short grass strip sloping down towards the sea at both ends. From the air it looked like an aircraft carrier made of rock. In 1770, Captain Cook named the area Cape Howe. The Aboriginal name is Gabo, and not surprisingly the island became known as Gabo Island.

In 1853, the steamship Monumental City was wrecked off the Cape with a loss of thirty-three lives and a decision was then made to build the lighthouse, with work completed in 1862. The airstrip was not completed until 1973, with goods previously arriving by sea and urgent supplies by helicopter. The strip was 1,800 feet long which made it short but proved to be more than adequate and although the Aztec was used as the primary aircraft, the Navajo, with its better brakes, had no difficulty either. The critical part of the operation was the strength of the wind and the subsequent take-off. Once halfway down the strip you were only going to do one of two things: go flying or go for a swim! The company ran a very efficient service and I cannot recall anybody ever missing out and diverting.

The lighthouse keeper was Graham Campbell, joined by his lovely wife Dot. While the supplies were unloaded, we were always welcomed like family and that included scones with jam freshly made by Dot. I have very fond memories of lazy days at Gabo, with the seals and fairy penguins. Graham would answer all his mail, and this could take some hours. After a stomach full of scones, I would often go for a walk around this beautiful island. Once I found a large blackberry bush full of ripe berries and had an impromptu feast. On returning to the lighthouse, Graham noticed my stained purple lips and looked aghast. "George, you lunatic," he said, "I sprayed those yesterday!" Fortunately, I have shown no signs of being affected by Graham's insecticide.

3.1 Piper PA23 Aztec VH-MBQ, Gabo Island, 1 December 1978.

Three graves existed on the island: two belonged to young children, one only 12 months old and the other 20 months. The third grave belonged to a young girl aged 24 with a different surname. All died in 1861 and are thought to be family members of the construction party. It does illustrate how tough the conditions must have been. Today the lighthouse is no longer manned, having been converted to an automatic station.

I was eventually approved to fly on the Premier's contract and this included flying the State Premier Dick Hamer. He sometimes flew in company with his wife, April, who had overly sensitive ears and wanted to stay down at low level. I flew them both to Echuca once, flying VFR through the busy light aircraft lane to the west of Melbourne and then racing along below the control zone. The Premier was a charming man, very gracious and always seemed to appreciate the trip. If he had known the lack of protection he had by flying outside controlled airspace with all the 'unknown' traffic about, he might have had second thoughts about his wife's discomfort.

Lindsay Thomson, the Minister for Education, was another regular customer; he suffered from airsickness and was extremely ill on occasions. Once going to Swan Hill in terrible weather he was ill all the way but still managed to pull himself together, stoically marching off with his minders to open a new school. I had great admiration for him, especially after an hour or so he would turn up for a repeat performance and never complain.

Regular charters for the oil industry would appear on the roster, completing the variety of work available. A gas blow-out on the Moomba pipeline resulted in an urgent request one night to send an engineering expert up at short notice. I was the last to arrive for the traditional Friday night drinks and Graeme rostered me to take him immediately. The other pilots took great delight in my obvious disappointment, one saying, "It pays to be early," another adding, "Sorry, George, I've had a drink!"

Arriving back empty the next morning over Moorabbin, I joined the circuit. When selecting the wheels down the right-hand side, this indicated a failure to lower. The tower confirmed this, and I asked to fly out into the training area to see if I could sort it out. Tom Biddell was the duty controller and he was very switched on. When he said I had only one belly door open, I knew I had a problem as the doors only open to allow the gear out and then are sequenced closed. Something had broken and all attempts to lower the offending leg using the emergency system proved futile. Having come all the way direct from Moomba (205 miles northeast of Leigh Creek), I was low on fuel, tired from flying all night and had to make up my mind quickly.

Peter Lang, the Chief Engineer, was consulted and by now a small crowd was gathering at the base of the tower. I decided to make a 'gear-up' landing on the small grass emergency strip – the only problem was while I managed to get all the gear up, the offending door refused to budge and still hung down. The gear sequence was still incomplete, and the damaged leg not locked up either. My main concern was the leg falling out as I was about to touch down, causing all sorts of problems. Tom, to his great credit, worked this out as well and without prompting, called out regularly the gear status as I approached to land.

The early Navajos had two bladed propellers, so I shut down the right engine, feathered the propeller and using the starter, positioned the blades horizontally. I was not game to do it on the other side, electing to land without flaps, including closing the cowl flaps to minimise damage. To judge it properly, I needed some power from the remaining engine. The aeroplane was now exceptionally aerodynamically 'clean' and during the flare, wanted to keep flying. All went well with the hanging door making contact first and coming off with a loud bang. The aircraft then slid gracefully to a stop on its belly with the airport fire-engine racing alongside trying to keep up. Leaving the aircraft quickly, I was met by a fireman with an axe who kept yelling, "Where's the battery?" I promised to tell him if he put the axe away and did not damage the aircraft.

Graeme and Peter Lang then arrived in the yellow safety car. The first thing Graeme did was to check I was okay. But Peter Lang just kept on saying, "Shit", and stared back at the aeroplane. Peter never swore, so something was really bothering him. It turned out that the right propeller only had a few hours left on it but the left one was brand new. I was not to know this and here was the right one without a scratch and the left one curled back like a banana! Graeme was pleased with the lack of overall damage and the aircraft was flying again within a few days. The cause of the failure was a fatigue failure of one of the door hinges, resulting in the broken hinge jamming the main gear door. Metal fatigue occurs when metal parts are weakened due to repeated stresses.

Microscopic cracks tend to form, especially around sharp edges and eventually lead to failure.

The State Electricity Commission contract was an air sampling one with a special probe fitted to one of the Navajos (VH-MBY), together with portable recording equipment carried in the cabin. Ross, the technician assigned to the project, became one of the team and even attended Friday night sessions. The new Yallourn Power Station required two giant cooling towers and our job was to find any temperature inversions in the Latrobe Valley that might cause unnecessary pollution. A trend or a 'history marker' was required to find any patterns unique to the area and we took air samples for months trying to determine the best position for the towers. The task took the form of flying in circles over a fixed spot on the ground and then climbing up in a spiral at 1,000-foot intervals, taking samples and then climbing to the next level and so on. It required accurate flying and, while on the surface, the job seemed a little dull, Ross was a very pleasant character and we somehow made it into a very productive and enjoyable exercise. During the trip home, we often gave Ross an unofficial flying lesson and today he is the proud owner of his own light aircraft, a kit-plane on floats.

It was during my time with AAC that I faced my greatest demons – passing the Senior Commercial or Airline Transport Pilot theory subjects. These examinations were well known as the cause of many careers to go no further and many pilots simply could not pass them. With my academic background this was going to be 'make or break' and I was determined that for once in my life, bookwork would not beat me. I became obsessed with the subject material, carrying it in my head wherever I went. I completed past exams and studied for hours daily, even reading my notes while flying. Some evenings I studied into the early hours with only four hours of sleep.

The exams were held in the Prahran Town Hall and supervised by an elderly and officious-looking member of the Department.

One interesting character I met in the entrance hall was an ex-Royal Navy pilot who had flown jets off aircraft carriers. We enjoyed some nervous pre-exam banter and he ended up in the seat directly in front of mine.

The Navigation plot required a track to be drawn across two charts, the problem being the charts were edged with a wide white margin, not to mention the fact the ruler was not long enough. I solved the problem by neatly folding over the margins and using the slide rule from my navigation plotter to extend the length of my ruler. The line may not have been perfectly straight, but it was workable.

It quickly became apparent that my Navy companion was under some stress and he attracted the attention of the supervisor by constantly muttering, "Bloody ridiculous!" Without any further warning, he yelled out, "Stuff it!" and stood up, promptly picking up the vacant desk in front of him, turning it upside down. With one fluid motion, he placed it on his two maps and used the table edge to draw his track line! The rest of the class immediately burst out laughing and he was frog-marched out of the examination room, shouting obscenities to the stern-faced official. Very amusing, I thought, and it greatly reduced the tension. I have often wondered how he went at the next sitting. To my great surprise, I passed all subjects.

Nothing comes easy as they say, because when I applied for my Senior Licence, I was advised that I would be one of the first candidates to be subjected to the new rule of a further flight test. The test for the Senior Commercial Licence was to be a VFR navigation exercise in a 'sophisticated retractable undercarriage aircraft.' Nobody seemed quite sure what this meant, but it appeared the humble Piper Aztec was suitable, and Graham Lowe very kindly allowed me free use of the company aircraft.

The Testing Officer was none other than John Lindsay. I considered John one of my favourites, but he only held a Commercial

Licence and was one of those people who for whatever reason had not passed his senior theory subjects. He was amused by all of this, especially testing me for a licence he did not hold himself and he gave me a simple exercise. The Department of Civil Aviation seemed to be a law to unto itself.

4
HEAVY TIME
1977–1978

When everything seems to be going against you, remember the airplane takes off against the wind, not with it.
Henry Ford

I enjoyed my years with Australian Air Charters and still feel it was some of the best flying of my career. The pay, however, was never going to be enough to sustain a normal lifestyle and my marriage was already starting to show cracks. We were living from hand to mouth with no prospects of saving money. I had applied for the airlines but was rejected by Qantas because I lacked mathematics at the required level. Both TAA and Ansett offered some hope but required 'experience commensurate with age.' After flying professionally for six years, I was fast approaching the cut-off age of 28 years. The airlines would consider you above this age, but you needed heavy aircraft time or at least turbine or jet time. A further brick wall was erected by the fact that neither company were recruiting at the time! It also goes without saying that to get a job flying larger aircraft or a jet, you needed experience in this field beforehand. I had been confronted by the 'impossible' before and knew I would find a way if I was just patient.

Sure enough, it came from a much unexpected quarter. On 10 May 1975 at 2.20am, Air Express Ltd of Essendon lost a Bristol Freighter cargo aircraft 17 miles south of Wonthaggi in Victoria. Under the command of Captain Les Barnes and in the company of a young Radio Operator, they were forced to ditch into Bass Strait after failing to maintain height following an engine failure. Both crew members lost their lives and little of the aircraft was recovered.

The Department, after more than a year of investigation, recommended, among other things, that aircraft weighing more than 12,500 lbs should have a crew of two pilots. Air Express had been flying with the second crew member, a Radio Operator, for some time and now required co-pilots to resume operations.

I applied immediately and after a short interview with the Manager, Derick Scott, and Chief Pilot Gordon Howe, I was offered one of the positions available. Gordon was previously an Examiner for the Department and had renewed my Instrument rating several times in the past. He was one of the instigators of the single pilot instrument rating and knowing my background, welcomed me aboard with open arms – a pleasant change for once.

At the time the company was merging with Brain and Brown, another freight operator which was equipped with the famous DC-3. I was offered either the Bristol or the DC-3 but chose the Bristol because it weighed 44,000 lbs all up weight compared to the DC-3 at 26,000 lbs. It is one of the decisions I have always regretted. At the time, my mind was on flying the heaviest aircraft I could get my hands on.

After a short ground school, I began my endorsement with Len Veager. The Bristol was very intimidating at first and seemed massive compared to the light twins I had been flying. It also was a 'tail dragger' where the main wheels were supported by a small tail wheel. Known in the old days as a 'conventional undercarriage', they had some limitations directionally as the weight of the aircraft is mainly aft of the main wheels. Any swing or change in direction is greatly magnified by the momentum behind the wheels and control, especially in cross winds, so it is more difficult. Any swing that is allowed to develop more than ten to twenty degrees can rapidly result in a ground-loop where the aircraft literally ends up facing the opposite direction. Few aircraft can take this side loading on the gear, and such a manoeuvre generally ends up with at least a wrecked undercarriage.

During World War II, nose wheels eliminated this characteristic and are now standard on all modern aircraft. I had tail-wheel time on a variety of aircraft but nothing of this size or power. With two sleeve-valve engines of 1980bhp, the aircraft could lift four tons of freight at a slightly slower speed compared with the DC-3 which carried a three-ton load. The company operated both the Bristol 170-21 and the 170-31. The Mark 31 had bigger engines with an increase in fin area via a dorsal fillet, spinners on the propellers and toe brakes but otherwise both types looked similar. The Mark 21 had the very English hand-operated brakes using a bicycle type lever on the control wheel. Once used to this oddity, I really liked it but toe brakes are the norm.

Entry to the cockpit was via a small hatch beneath the nose. The hatch released by turning the handle and hung down suspended from the rear. On the inside of the hatch, two toe-holes enabled the crew member to climb up into the nose section which was known as compartment A. The heavy over-centre locks holding the large clam shell nose cargo doors were all very carefully checked and then it was a climb up a ladder fixed to the starboard cargo wall to enter the cockpit through the cockpit floor. The job of the co-pilot was to then climb out of the cockpit roof via a roof hatch to check the oil. The oil tanks were to the rear and on top of the engine nacelles. We achieved this with the aid of a wooden dipstick but walking on the steeply sloping wing at night required some care. The oil tanks contained no less than 20 gallons of oil with the aircraft's engines consuming some 3 gallons an hour, an extraordinary amount by today's jet standards.

4.1 Bristol Freighter Mk31 VH-ADL Air Express, October 1977. Photo taken by David Carter.

4.2 Bristol Freighter MK21 RAAF Museum Pt Cook.

4.3 Bristol Freighter MK 21 cockpit VH-SJG November 1977.

The Bristol's cockpit was straight out of World War II, basic but functional. A large Sperry Autopilot dominated the centre instrument panel complete with a lever, not unlike an undercarriage lever, and marked ON and OFF. Three large tuning knobs allowed the Autopilot indices to be trimmed in roll, pitch and yaw prior to engagement. The whole contraption was pneumatically powered and despite its primitive appearance worked quite well. The tall 'T' shaped throttles were coloured red for port and green for starboard, handy, I suppose, if you have trouble remembering your left from right. The pitch levers for the propellers and two friction nuts were coloured in a similar fashion. In place of mixture controls were Carby Shut-off Valves marked OFF and RUN. One of the unique features of the Bristol was automatic mixture control. The primers and starters were on a small panel to the left of the captain's knee.

First engaging the starter, we counted out aloud the number of blades passing the cockpit window. On the seventh, primer buttons were hit, then on the ninth, ignition ON and the engine came to life only as a large radial can. Smoke rose around the cowl and under the watchful eye of a ground engineer, ready with a fire extinguisher, the engine began to clear into a distinct crackle from the stub exhausts.

Due to the delay in the pneumatic brakes, taxiing was not as easy as I thought it should be and it took several hours before I mastered it. The secret was to apply both brakes together and then one more than the other to achieve directional change. To apply one brake only tended to cause over controlling. One eye had also to be kept on the split pressure gauge. As I gained more experience, asymmetric power helped to turn in tight spaces and opposite engine power to prevent any 'over swing.' The aircraft was also fitted with an electrical tail wheel lock; you first had to taxi in a straight line and then on selecting the switch, a solenoid dropped a pin into two aligned holes. With a restriction of five minutes or you could burn it out, it was, to say the least, unusual in a world of mechanical locks.

The Mark 31 was registered VH-ADL and named by the company as the Tasmanian Devil; the crews however preferred Adolf and it seemed an apt name. When taxiing out with the sun behind you, the shadow ahead resembled a strange beast with the brakes hissing and squealing and the engines crackling away.

Due to the automatic mixture control, the throttle quadrant was marked with the ECB range (Economical, Cruise and Boost). During take-off, it was not permitted to pause at this setting in order to avoid too lean a fuel mixture – you had to quickly push through this range to take-off power. This often caused an early swing to develop, especially as the tail was coming up. It took some anticipation and judgement to not only catch it but avoid over-controlling. The noise on take-off could only be described as painful; it did, in fact, physically hurt and communication was only possible with hand signals or by shouting through the intercom. Once airborne, the aircraft climbed with the strange sensation of a lift with the nose 'nodding' in any turbulence. The controls were heavy but overall, the aircraft was easy to fly.

The landing was another matter. With what felt like solid rubber blocks in the undercarriage, any back pressure on initial touchdown resulted in the aircraft bouncing vigorously back into the air and the subsequent skips took some forward stick to pin the aircraft down. I flew with several older captains who mastered the three-pointer landings with great skill but I preferred the 'wheel-landing', lowering the tail down gently. Once the bounce was fully understood, it seemed the easier option.

I soon settled into my new job and flew mainly to Tasmania and King Island. Flying at night during the winter months proved daunting as we were forced to fly extremely low to avoid icing, having no anti-icing equipment. It was not uncommon to be as low as 1500 feet, the lowest safe altitude, while crossing the Bass Strait. I can still remember those heaving swells foaming with white caps clearly visible in the moonlight and watching the engine gauges anxiously. Here again, the aircraft had a strange quirk, every now and then one engine would completely miss a beat with a very distinct 'thump'. We called this the 'the Bristol cough', and no explanation of this was ever given despite heavy discussions with the ground engineers. After a 'cough' we would always make eye contact with each other and smile but nevertheless it was disconcerting.

We flew general cargo, including fresh fish northbound but were also capable of carrying two cars. In Europe the Mark 32 Bristol became a successful car ferry across the English Channel with a company called Silver City Airways. With an extended nose section, the Mark 32 could carry three cars but none of this version ever operated in Australia. Within the cargo hold we carried two steel ramps, and to load a car these were fixed onto the nose sill and the car driven up the ramps through the open nose doors. To measure the width of the cars' wheelbase we used a notched broom handle and then adjusted the ramps accordingly (crude but effective). We could load a car and have it chained to the floor in fifteen minutes or less. Another fascinating loading system was the turnstile at the abattoirs on King Island. By placing a wheel on the concrete turnstile, the aircraft could be quickly rotated to face an elevated rail. This rail would then be extended into the aircraft nose and sides of beef could be loaded in a matter of seconds.

Backloads of fish were common and so were sacks of scheelite, a rare mineral heavier than lead and mined on the island. A near disaster was narrowly avoided when a load of scheelite and a load of furniture were inadvertently loaded together. The dispatcher had mistakenly thought the aircraft was empty due to the weight of the scheelite producing only a thin layer over the floor space. The crew became suspicious during the walk-around by the shape of the bottom of the tyres which seemed flatter than normal. The opinion of most was the aircraft may have got the tail up upon take-off but probably would not have flown. Due to the relative short length of the strip, an accident of some sort would have been inevitable.

One night after arriving at Essendon from Launceston with a load of fish, I noticed during landing a large fire burning in the direction of Melbourne's Tullamarine Airport. A quick look at my watch made my heart sink; it was the exact time my old company should be departing on the paper run. On climbing down from the cockpit, I was met by a ground engineer. Looking at his face, I knew there had been an accident. "Sorry, George; it was one of your old mob and it looks very bad."

News in aviation travels fast and I quickly learned that Peter Benton had experienced an engine fire on take-off and had crashed off the end of the runway near the old people's home. He had made a valiant attempt at a forced landing but had been overcome by a fierce fire after one wing clipped a tree dislodging and rupturing a main fuel line.

I drove home via Moorabbin and met some of my fellow pilots there, and will never forget the sadness. To see Peter's car in the car park, knowing he would never return, was a terrible experience. Two months later, one of the instructors at my original job with

Peninsula Air Services, John Fleming, was also killed trying to avoid a thunderstorm and for the first time in my life I felt like giving flying away. Time heals all, as they say, and we all tried to move on. It turned out that the failure was only a hole in a piston and the Department in their report insinuated Peter prematurely shut down an engine that was still capable of limited power. We all resented these 'experts' who, I might add, took weeks to come to these lofty conclusions. Peter, with an aircraft not even fitted with an engine fire extinguisher, had only seconds to decide. He also could not see the approaching ground; the Navajo had landing lights fixed on the undercarriage and with the wheels retracted he was literally blind. I was learning a lot about 'pilot error', something that seems to happen if you are not around to defend yourself.

4.4 *The loss of Peter Benton, 30 March 1978, Navajo Chieftain VH-MBK. CASA Safety Digest.*

After a year at Air Express, I was selected to convert on to the DC-4 and began my ground school, which was run by Qantas, the former owners of the aircraft. The Qantas instructor was 'very Qantas', immaculately dressed and correct in bearing. He seemed horrified at this group of students in their jeans and roll-neck sweaters lounging in the back of the engine shop. This was our makeshift classroom, complete with drums of oil and dirty rags hanging off empty fish bins. I must admit, I rather enjoyed his displeasure and we kept up the appearance by being as rough as possible!

Despite the quiet animosity between students and instructor, we all passed the course and I looked forward to flying the four-engine DC-4. It was not to be. We were shocked to hear the very next day that the company was in trouble and half the crews would be laid off almost immediately. I was to be one of them. The company had lost a court case against the Two Airline Policy which effectively prevented any heavy aircraft operator from operating a regular service in competition. It was a great disappointment. Graham Lowe offered me my old job back so at least I could pay my bills but for the first time in my career, it felt like I was going backward.

I quickly settled back into my old routine and began to consider going overseas, a path that seemed to offer more prospects than Australia. Several friends had already chosen this route and I was constantly being regaled with stories of fast jets and equally fast women. Mark Beville-Anderson, a pilot and friend from my Point Cook days, was now flying a CASA 212 turboprop in Libya in support of the oil industry. Mark had an unpleasant experience when one of his passengers was killed instantly when he blundered down the wrong side of the aircraft and walked through a rotating propeller. The authorities wanted to arrest Mark and charge him with manslaughter, and he was lucky to escape the country. I had travelled extensively as a child and was more cautious of the 'grass is greener' syndrome.

5
CONNAIR DARWIN
1979–1981

"It's a pass but you are still very GA."
Stan McGrath, Check Captain, 22 April 1980

An advertisement appeared one day for Connair; the Northern Territory Airline founded by aviation pioneer Eddie Connellan. While the company had a motley fleet of light aircraft, DC-3s and de Havilland Herons (a four-engine regional airliner), they held a coveted Regular Public Transport licence. Industry rumour strongly suggested that they would be bought out by one of the major players. This was an opportunity too good to miss and I applied straight away. Following a comprehensive interview, unlike anything I had experienced before, which included a handwriting test, I was delighted to learn I had been accepted. My marriage was almost over, so it seemed a good chance for a trial separation. Now that I was the father of a young daughter, it was with great sadness that I left the family home in Melbourne and headed for Darwin in the Northern Territory.

Darwin, on my arrival in January 1979, had made a remarkable recovery after being virtually destroyed by Cyclone Tracy on Christmas Day 1974. Large areas of the suburbs still had tell-tale signs of the destruction, with concrete slabs the only reminder that this was once somebody's home. The twisted telegraph poles, or Stobie Poles as they are called, are still etched into my memory. Made of concrete and steel, the concrete had all but disappeared and the remaining parallel steel supports were literally twisted around each other into grotesque shapes. It defied imagination that such damage could be caused by the wind. The town itself had mostly been rebuilt and there was a noticeable 'can-do' spirit about the place.

5.1 Navajo Chieftain.

I was assigned initially to the General Aviation side of the company, operating familiar Navajo Chieftains. The primary task was a twice-daily run, servicing the uranium mine at Narbalek. Gordon Mills, aka Gundy, was the pilot in charge, and with my very General Aviation background we clicked instantly. Gundy was another of those pilots without his Senior Subjects, operating on a Commercial Licence. I never asked why, but assumed he had attempted and failed at some stage. He was very bitter about it and showed some animosity towards the airline side and the pilots who were operating on Airline Transport Pilot Licences. In those days, you had to be employed by an airline to hold an ATPL and even then, co-pilots operated on a Second-Class Licence and captains held a First Class. Outside the airline system, if you flew a heavy aircraft, you would operate on a Senior Commercial Licence. A bare Commercial Licence restricted you to aircraft below 12,500 lbs or 5700 kg categorised as light aircraft.

When I was flying with Gundy to assess my ability, it soon became apparent he was 'old school' and he gave me a comprehensive work-out, including steep turns just a few feet above a line of coconut trees. While I agree with the critics who claim this is dangerous and unnecessary, I could see where he was coming from and said nothing. I was rewarded with a "you'll do" which I considered a compliment after some of the comments I heard from other pilots.

Following a few trips to the Narbalek Mine it soon became obvious that I was expected to convert to the Heron and fly as a co-pilot on the airline routes. On one hand, I wanted the ATPL but on the other I preferred the single-pilot charter flying.

The Heron weighed 13,500 lbs and carried 16 passengers but to me never had the feel of a heavy aeroplane, especially after my experience with the Bristol. The cockpit was extremely cramped, it almost seemed that the designer forgot about the pilots and the cockpit was an add-on, appearing as a bulge at the end of the fuselage. The cockpit door was shaped like the lid of a coffin, being wider at the top to allow for easier access. This always looked a little ominous to me. The Heron was re-engined from the originals and fitted with the same IO 540 Lycoming engines of the Piper Navajo. The turbochargers were removed which de-rated the engine to 290hp. This modification from the original Gypsy engines was technically referred to as a Riley Heron, but nobody called them that.

Built as a 'feeder airliner' in the early fifties, the aircraft had all the British features of this era: bag-pneumatic brakes, fabric control surfaces and other oddities. The fuel cross-feed selector was positioned behind the captain's seat, an awkward position. It was impossible to reach without releasing your shoulder harness. The flaps only had two positions: 20 degrees or 'down', with 'down' being no less than 60 degrees which gave the aircraft slow approach speeds for a relatively steep nose-down attitude. One duty of the co-pilot was to try and keep all four engines synchronised via four electrical switches accompanied with four blue lights, an almost unachievable task as any speed or pitch change would leave the engines back out of synch again.

5.2 DeHavilland DH114 Heron of Conair. Photo taken by David Carter.

I found it difficult to adapt to the rigid 'airline style' of flying – every action and procedure was to be the same all the time. Commonly called Standard Operating Procedures or SOPs, it seemed vastly different to my natural freelance style of single pilot operations. I quickly realised that if I wanted a career in this more disciplined form of flying, I would have to adapt. I passed my line training but was disappointed to be graded only as average. I was written up as being 'very GA' – General Aviation. This tickled Gundy no end and he requested my services back on the charter side. The result was a nice balance of both charter and airline sectors on my roster.

The Heron was used primarily to service the many Aboriginal settlements throughout the Northern Territory. Destinations included Snake Bay and Garden Point on Melville Island, Bathurst Island, Croker, Goulburn and Elcho Islands and Gove on the Nhulunbuy Peninsula. To the south we flew to Tindal, to the east, Maningrida. The terrain can only be described as spectacular, especially through the Kakadu National Park and the Alligator Rivers.

During the dry season, hundreds of thousands of magpie geese take over the area, joining cockatoos, white egrets and whistler ducks. Feral pigs and water buffalo abounded on the flood plains, although after I left the Territory, the government decided to kill off the buffaloes due to the damage they were causing to the environment.

I never tired of flying over this region. The Alligator Rivers, the West, South and East Alligator, were all named by an Englishman, Philip Parker King, who mistook the local crocodiles for alligators! I suppose you cannot blame him for not studying them more closely, as some were true monsters measuring over 20 feet in length. On hearing the aircraft, they would slide off the mud flats into the river and all you would see were body slide prints and a great cloud of muddy water. On the few occasions I flew back from the Narbarlek Mine devoid of passengers, I would throttle back and quietly glide low over the river to catch them unawares, basking on the mud banks. It was an eerie sight to see the ground come alive as they moved for the safety of the water. Sometimes you would spot a large croc swimming offshore in Chambers Bay. I have seen them as much as a mile off the beach just cruising along.

Dugongs and giant black and white mantra rays were also common, although sightings of sharks were rare. Packs of dingos and even wild horses were not uncommon either – all in all a fascinating area. During the wet season, afternoon storms presented particularly challenging flying weather and once again we were initially without weather radar.

One event I remember fondly around this time was the day Gundy approached me walking towards the aircraft in an out of character state of apprehension. He quickly told me that he was in deep trouble; the Department of Transport (as DCA was now called) wanted the company to rewrite the GA Operations Manual to be compliant with new regulations. Apart from not knowing what the new regulations were, or the old ones for that matter, he said he had not a clue on how to go about it and asked if I would help him. I told him I would talk about it on my return over a beer and he still looked dejected as I taxied out. I concluded that I had no idea either but that night I sat down in the Darwin Hotel with him and after a few beers decided that somehow, I would do it for him.

I bought a copy of the Air Navigation Orders and a copy of the Air Navigation Regulations. We sat down together and made a list of all the requirements and subject matter to be listed in an operating manual. I then made up all the relevant chapters and sections and prepared to write it up in some sort of order. During this later stage, around at Gundy's house, we opened a bottle of Scotch for 'inspiration.' I decided that we must use the same 'official speak' and inserted many 'subject to' and 'in pursuant of'.

In a more sober state of mind the next day when I had completed it, I told Gundy that we might have "over-cooked it" and had doubts about handing it in. He had enough of all this and handed it in anyway. I spent an anxious week worrying about it and began to think about the consequences of making fun of the establishment. To my amazement, the Department not only accepted the manual but were full of praise for the 'professional job.' To Gundy's great credit he told Pat Harrison, the Operations Manager, that the work was mine and the company sent around a carton of beer and a letter of appreciation. Gundy and I had a great laugh about it all and felt proud that we had, to use Gundy's great grasp of the Aussie language, "out bullshitted the bullshitters."

After I had been with Connair for a few months, rumours began to do the rounds of a take-over from East-West Airlines, a regional operator based in Tamworth, New South Wales. The take-over did in fact occur that year and as with all negotiations of this nature the two pilot groups became embroiled in a bitter struggle for supremacy. The East-West pilots, not unnaturally, expected the Connair pilots to go to the bottom of the combined seniority list. This would effectively remove every command in Connair and relegate everyone as a First Officer.

The result, happily, was Connair being re-named Northern Airlines and kept as a separate identity. Our jobs were safe and not only that, but the new company was also awarded the Coastal Surveillance contract from the Federal Government. This contract was to be flown with the locally produced GAF Nomad, a twin-engine turbine-powered aircraft. Turbine-time was another vital stepping-stone for career advancement. It goes without saying that you could not move into the higher paying turbine jobs without turbine time and you needed a turbine job to get it, a familiar Catch 22. However, this was now going to be handed to me on a plate!

The company was also to fly the Nomad on the Northern Territory Aerial Medical Service contract. I was selected for the surveillance side and commenced a ground school for the engine handling of the Allison B250-17 engine. This included passing a Basic Gas Turbine exam set by the Department of Transport. After my experiences with these multi-choice examinations, I took to the task with 'head down and bum up' to an extent that even surprised Gundy. After refusing an invitation for the usual drinking session in the Darwin Hotel's Green Room, he expressed the opinion that I was "in danger of turning into an airline wanker." (This was a crude expression common in the industry where general aviation pilots resented their airline compatriots.)

5.3 *GAF N22 Nomad Searchmaster. Photo taken by David Carter.*

I passed the Gas Turbine examination, and this was followed by a two-day ground school on the aircraft systems and a Very Low Frequency Omega Navigation course conducted by Civil Flying Services of Melbourne. On the first inspection of the real aircraft, it seemed large for its weight of 8400 lbs, with the tail standing more than 18 feet from the ground. Access to the cockpit was via an external step and a climb up the side of the fuselage. Opening the cockpit door revealed a spacious crew area more akin to a helicopter cockpit with extensive glazing. Two non-adjustable red webbing seats looked crude by modern standards but proved to be surprisingly comfortable. The right-hand seat was unavailable for passenger use as it came within a direct line of the propeller arc, an odd design flaw that one would have thought must have been obvious to its designers. (Disappointing to learn that the regulators thought it was okay for the pilot to be chopped up by a malfunctioning propeller.)

The aircraft proved throughout its relatively short history to be a controversial machine. Several were lost to accidents early in its development, including a crash at Avalon in Victoria which killed not only the GAF's chief test pilot Stuart Pearce but also the assistant head designer. Like all controversial subjects, some facts were lost in sensational press reports and sadly some accidents were simply plain old pilot error. I personally found the aircraft pleasant enough to fly but there is no doubt it had its peculiarities. One of the more unusual design features was in roll control – the aircraft was equipped with standard ailerons, but these were directly connected to the flaps. As the flaps were lowered the ailerons became part of a full span double slotted flap, the roll control being replaced by overwing spoilers. This rather complicated sequence was controlled by an intricate system of chains and pulleys that at first glance seemed to be borrowed from a bicycle. The result for the pilot was a light roll response with the flaps up but as they progressively lowered to the full 40 degrees, the roll control became very heavy and a little unwieldy. Like most high wing aircraft with powerful flaps, the Nomad had a steep nose-down attitude during the approach and a surprisingly quick loss of airspeed if the power was reduced too rapidly. ("More drag than a gay bar," according to Gundy.) The landing distance was short and reverse thrust could be used for even more impressive results. Due to wear on the gearbox, we seldom used reverse. The take-off performance, like all aircraft, was greatly affected by the heat and we were normally limited by the engine temperature limits, not the engine torque limit.

Here again, during the take-off run, the aircraft displayed an interesting control response. Reaching the take-off safety speed, a sensible pull back on the control column produced no reaction, increasing the amount of back pressure. This resulted in the aircraft suddenly pitching into the air, and forward pressure was required to maintain the correct climb attitude. Once these quirks were understood, the aircraft was straightforward enough and not nearly as bad as some of the stories that followed its tainted history.

We were equipped with two models for the surveillance task, the N22L Search Master and the N22B. The 'L' was fitted with a large 'chin' radar made by Litton fitted underneath the nose and the 'B' had the Bendix radar fitted internally giving the extreme nose a 'thimble' appearance and was the more aesthetic of the two. The Litton radar was operated by a dedicated radar operator who sat in the dark behind a curtained-off area, ably assisted by an observer who would take photographs of the subject matter with a camera. This would record the latitude and longitude on the print for use as evidence. The Litton-equipped aircraft would fly the ocean surveillance and the Bendix equipped aircraft would simply fly along the coastline with two observers looking for illegal activities.

We completed a course on ship recognition which I found most interesting, learning the differences between a Ketch, a Sloop and all the varieties of trawlers. We were taught how to 'rig' a vessel for the purpose of either taking a photograph or simply reading the name on the hull. We were not allowed to cross the bow or overfly the vessel, one being the international distress signal and the other to avoid colliding with aerials or other protrusions. The technique was to fly along the vessel's length on the starboard side from stern to bow. Using a radar altimeter, we were trained in low flying and approved to operate down to 50 feet using the radar altimeter warning light, set to 50 feet, exactly to our limit.

The low flying flight test was conducted by an ex-Army pilot, Vic Salmon, who had flown during the Vietnam War. Vic was a Department of Transport Examiner and I remember him eyeing me suspiciously prior to the test. He quickly had me flying at 50 feet with instructions to follow the Adelaide River without crossing any of the banks. This I found just possible but on one S-bend it was the poor roll control of the Nomad that was nearly my undoing. I just made it! Rolling wings level and climbing away steeply, I glanced over to Vic and he was grinning like the Cheshire Cat (all in a day's work for an Army aviator). Vic would later join Ansett and retired as a 767 Captain.

I thought the work was interesting for a while, especially the coastal run with its wildlife, and even more interesting, the many old, World War II aircraft wrecks. However, like all things of routine, especially when nothing was sighted, it became quite boring and I preferred the ocean run where we would seek out the shipping right out to Australia's maritime boundary.

It was while doing the ocean surveillance I was once presented with a 'chip' warning light on the left engine which indicated contamination in the left gearbox. The procedure was to shut the engine down but in view of our distance offshore, I had a quick discussion with the other crew members, and we agreed to close some of the distance to the coast first. Tracking directly towards Bathurst Island, we had no sooner contacted the company when the right engine also came up with a chip warning light. There was no point in doing anything now but to wait and see what other engine indications developed.

When this information was passed on to the company, some comedian on the company frequency said, "Can I have your car?" The lucky result was that these warnings were false with the engineers saying a sticky deposit was fouling the chip detectors. This problem persisted for a few months until the engineers found a solution. At the time, sitting a hundred miles offshore, with two engines that supposedly were about to fail was quite worrying, especially with the Timor Sea being so unfriendly. On numerous occasions we spotted packs of sea snakes all tangled together in raft-like formations and clouds of jelly-fish, not to mention the sharks. The Radar Operator gave a loud cheer when we crossed the coast of Bathurst Island but was subdued when I reminded him that the ground below was crocodile country, and we were not out of the woods yet. By now I was convinced both warnings were false but there was no harm in prolonging his agony!

Graham Mowbray, who not only completed my endorsement but had also accompanied me during a delivery flight from the factory, asked if I would like to be a training pilot. I agreed to this promotion and ended up training two of my former Heron captains on the Nomad operation. Both, I must admit, took to the task most graciously and any awkwardness was quickly removed. I gained great respect for them, especially when Stan McGrath said, "I was always told to be nice to your co-pilot because one day he could be your captain." Throughout my career I have seen this situation happen more than a few times.

Stan was lucky to be alive following a tragic accident on Melville Island. While unloading some freight, Larry, his co-pilot drove the delivery truck at him as a joke. The truck's brakes either failed or Larry misjudged the distance and Stan was crushed between the truck and the aircraft fuselage. To Larry's great credit, he loaded the injured pilot onto the aircraft and single-handedly flew Stan to Darwin for urgent medical treatment. Stan made a full recovery and never felt or showed any animosity toward his co-pilot. It goes without saying that Larry never forgave himself and seemed to carry his guilt wherever he went, and became very withdrawn.

During this time, my wife made contact and expressed a wish for us to have another try at our marriage. Since I was missing my young daughter, I agreed and for a while we were a happy family again, moving into a flat in the northern suburb of Casuarina. However dark clouds were soon on the horizon as reports began to filter down that the company was in trouble. Within weeks the company did indeed collapse, but it looked like Ansett would take over the RPT runs, and the Aerial Medical contract, and eligible pilots would be able to transfer over to Ansett.

6
ANSETT TAKE-OVER
1981

"Fail anything twice and you're out!"
Ansett Ground Instructor, April 1981

Once again, I was on the move, this time back to Melbourne. The age limit agreed to was 32 or below, and this thinned our ranks considerably. Those remaining were subjected to a full day of aptitude tests by the Melbourne firm Chandler-McCleod. With a noticeable tension in the air, we all filed into the Astro-Jet building at Tullamarine Airport, sat in long rows with the desks set apart to avoid cheating and once again I tried to convince the head shrinkers I was not insane or lacking basic intelligence. We never received any results, but I passed and began the long process of induction into the Ansett system.

Ground school on the Fokker F-27 Friendship commenced at a pace I immediately found taxing. The aircraft seemed unnecessarily complicated compared to the Nomad. The propeller alone required a full day of lectures followed by an exam the following morning. Modern propellers, especially on larger turbine aircraft, are extremely powerful. In simple terms, the propeller is a rotating wing using the same basic aerodynamic principles. Massive amounts of torque must be controlled in the event of a loss of propeller control. This is accomplished with a system of locks. The propeller was fitted with two locks for protection, one low pitch lock and one high pitch lock. The pilots monitored the locking mechanism by a system of lights – blue lights for the flight safety lock set at 32 degrees, orange lights for the Prop Below Lock, if the blades got below 18 degrees. On the right-hand side of the panel, two red lights or circuit condition lights monitored Flight Safe and Flight Fine.

With all this explained in rapid succession, I just sat there with a dumb look of disbelief. There was so much to remember; the flight safety lock came in automatically when both props exceeded 34 degrees and out again when both were below 34 degrees or with one feathered. It could be withdrawn manually by placing the High-Pressure Cock to manual. The whole system had several emergency scenarios requiring a full understanding, including memorising checklists. I left the classroom that evening quite demoralised. It was only by burning the midnight oil and going through it all several times that I managed to pass the exam the next morning.

The engines were no less complicated, and every take-off required some adjustments. They were unlike modern engines, with their Electronic Engine Control or even the earlier Power Management Control which afforded various protections for the pilot. The Rolls-Royce Dart engines on the Fokker Friendship offered no such luxury and required constant manual adjustments. Calibrated for maximum power in a test cell they were then fitted with a data card and a pedestal card. Each card had the Water Methanol Check Pressure, the Min Dry PWR (Minimum Dry Power) and Min TQE (Minimum Torque). Corrections for this basic data had to be applied for altitude above sea level and changes in temperature.

For example, the correction for Dry Power was to subtract 8 psi per 1,000 feet above sea level and 3 psi per 1 degree above International Standard Atmosphere (which is a base datum of 15 degrees C at sea level). Using the assistance of Water Methanol, 6 psi per 1000 feet above sea level had to be subtracted from the WMCP figure. Not less than minimum dry power had to be reached within 10 seconds of take-off power being set and not more than minimum dry plus 60 and so on.

Compared to the Nomad which had a fixed TGT (Turbine Gas Temperature) or Torque limit on take-off, this all seemed extremely difficult to me. To make the Nomad even simpler, in the hot tropics we were always temperature limited and that limit was the only figure to remember. The Friendship seemed like a flying nightmare to me and I had trouble thinking anybody could work it all out in the short time available and actually go flying.

6.1 F27 Ansett Airlines of New South Wales, VH-FCE, Mascot, Sydney, June 1981. Photo taken by David Carter.

After almost two months of Link, ground school and general induction, we were finally ready to commence the aircraft endorsement program. The rosters were issued, and I was surprised to discover that I was to fly as a passenger to Cairns and commence the endorsement the next day at Cairns airport. In the company of Bob Mahon, another ex-Connair pilot, we flew up to Cairns in a DC-9. I found it interesting to note that on the scheduled return flight the aircraft blew the left engine and remained stranded in Cairns during our training.

After a sleepless night, Bob and I finally met our instructor in the hotel foyer, Captain Pat Feeny. We both knew how vital this part of our training was, as this was the first of many ways to get the chop; fail this and we were out. Pat seemed a pleasant enough fellow but a little aloof. I was beginning to realise that most of the staff, so far, had treated us with a strange mixture of sympathy and complete indifference, due to our status as one-stripe trainees. 'Boggies' is what they called us, a throwback from the Air Force for a Pilot Officer, the lowest of the Commissioned ranks. For an ex-LAC (Leading Aircraftman) it was water off a duck's back.

The journey to the airport went without much conversation. Bob and I tossed a coin to see who would go first; I lost. Arriving in the airport car-park, we spotted the aircraft sitting on the ramp. With tall skinny undercarriage legs, a long slim fuselage that seemed to hug the ground and a large tail, it looked almost bird-like in appearance. Weighing in at 20 tons it could only be a man-made bird, another failed attempt to copy nature. Would we be able to tame this beast?

With a mixture of excitement and anxiety we walked over (no security in those days) to begin the lesson. Pat led us around the outside explaining all the vents, aerials and other parts of the walk-around. We stood under the engine nacelle and observed the water-meth tank to the rear and the position of the undercarriage locks and pins. Additionally, control locks to prevent the controls moving uncommanded in the wind had to be removed. These simple devices were often nothing more than two flat wooden plates that fitted over and under the control surface and were referred to as cleats. The cleats for the control locks had to be removed before flight with the aid of a large pole fitted with a hand grip due to the height of the wing above the ground. A pair of adjustable grips was positioned on the other end. The pitot cover on the wing tip also had to be removed, being particularly awkward to grip with a wavering pole. (The pitot was a probe that measured static and dynamic pressure for airspeed instruments and was very vulnerable to contamination. Wasps loved them for nest building, and it was important to keep a cover on them when not in use). My clumsy first attempts waving the pole like a wand caused Pat to give me a puzzled look, as if to say, "God, we've got a right one here." I had to force myself to slow down and take a deep breath; this was not making a good impression!

Once inside the aircraft I felt more comfortable. After all, this is what I did for a living, it was only another aeroplane. In no time Pat was explaining the engine start sequence, then electrics came online, lights flashed and with the clicking of the igniters in the background we began to start the engines. Compared to the Nomad the propellers looked like windmills, slashing away just outside the cockpit window. The Rolls-Royce Darts howled with a high pitch shrill that was painful. They did not call this the 20-ton dog whistle for nothing.

Bob elected to go first, and I was instructed to do a take-off data card and manual load sheet. The take-off data card is simply a clip-on form with all the take-off figures extracted from a cockpit performance manual. The load sheet is a weight and balance calculation which includes trim and flap settings. All had been covered in ground school and although painfully slow, both tasks proved just within my capabilities. The first officer was responsible for the pressurisation and I monitored Bob as he turned off the ground blower and pre-set the manual controls for flight. In no time we were on our way, tucking up the gear in a sharp left turn to avoid the town and more importantly, the rapidly rising terrain. Pat went on to demonstrate the basic handling techniques, and after Bob had a go it soon became my turn to change seats.

I found the aircraft heavy in roll control, light in pitch and the rudder loads somewhere in between; not particularly well balanced. Procedures still seemed overly complicated – I suddenly felt mentally overloaded as Pat went from one drill to another. It was with some relief we returned to Cairns for circuits, both completing two touch and go landings. The aircraft was easy enough to land, although sitting so low to the ground, the eye height was something familiar to our previous experience and I think this helped. Pat acknowledged that we had achieved a good standard and I ended up confident that we would pass the endorsement. The final exercises were to be completed over the following day.

The next morning, we began learning to fly the aircraft on one engine. As the aircraft was fitted with a tall and powerful rudder, asymmetric flight proved no more difficult than previous types, but the rudder loads were physically high. We completed several in-flight shutdowns and re-lights, going through the emergency recall drills and trying to get it all word perfect. In the airline world, it seemed the words were just as important as the deeds. We both knew all was going well when Pat took control, and we had a quick look at Green Island from low level. "Looking for talent," as Pat called it. One fisherman who appeared to be waving with only two fingers was the only talent sighted and we returned for a landing. We followed up with night circuits which I enjoyed; I have always felt comfortable at night, for some reason, often producing more accurate flying. On the final landing Pat welcomed us to the fleet, and off to the pub we went!

After we returned to Melbourne, a week passed before the company administration finally caught up with us. I was disappointed to learn that I would be transferred to Airlines of New South Wales, based in Sydney. The cost of accommodation in Sydney ruled out the family joining me. Not only that, but the company also indicated that a further move was on the cards. With a pay-scale half my previous job, cracks began to emerge in the marriage again and once more I left the family home with mixed feelings to set up shop in Sydney.

I quickly teamed up with an ex-RAAF pilot, Rod Trower, renting an apartment together in the trendy inner-city neighbourhood of Paddington. Living next door was the female comedian Jeanie Little, whose claim to fame was dressing up in green garbage bags (Glad-Bags). Living among the gay bars of Oxford Street and all the weird alternative shops, Rod and I felt we had moved to another planet.

Unlike Melbourne, where the pace seemed quite leisurely, ANSW were keen to get us through the system as quickly as possible. I was assigned a training Captain, Ken Guimelli, a colourful ex-Ansett flying-boat pilot. Ansett operated a flying-boat service out of Rose Bay until the early seventies, flying mainly to Lord Howe Island. Some say this was the last of the good old romantic days of aviation and Ken still lived up to the image with a bashed hat and a delightful sense of fun. We hit it off immediately.

My first trip under training was typical of the 'milk runs' ANSW flew around the country towns, Sydney to Coonabarabran, Coonamble, Walgett, return to Coonabarabran and back to Sydney. Flying time, four hours and five minutes but a duty time of over eight hours.

The First Officer was responsible for the load sheet, the passenger manifest, the mail, pre-flight inspections, battery cart connection and even closing the passenger door prior to departure. Coupled with all the normal flying duties, procedures and weather forecasts, I found the work demanding to say the least. There always seemed too much to do and no time to do it, all the while the captain could be found leaning up against the fence chatting away with the passengers or ground staff.

Most of the country towns only had a Non-Directional-Beacon let-down, considered a non-precision approach aid and hard work, especially at night where a low-level circling approach had to be conducted once visual to line up with the runway. Cooma was particularly bad, the NDB being located well off the airfield resulting in a low-level visual track back to the field. With low cloud and darkness, the trick was to stay visual or a missed approach had to be commenced immediately.

The local captains had been with the company for many years, some bidding to avoid promotion to jets because of the lifestyle and simply because the job was more personal. Everybody knew everybody and, in some ways, it was like being a member of an exclusive club. The company even had a pet cat at Merimbula where the two flight attendants would have cat food at the ready as soon as the aircraft was parked. At Broken Hill, fresh milk and newspapers were smuggled to the Flight Service Operators, who in those days controlled the flight plans and radio services around country airports. Happy banter between the cabin crew and the pilots could be distracting, with practical jokes the order of the day. Some of the antics would warrant a jail term in these days of political correctness but we got the job done and worked with a level of efficiency that had to be seen to be believed.

After two months of training, I was signed off as having finished my training (cleared to the line) after passing my check-ride with Chief Pilot Nev Lavers. The flight consisted of a day trip to Merimbula and Cooma and a night sector to Dubbo where low cloud forced a tighter than normal circuit and I managed to overshoot the centreline to the runway, turning steeply to get back in position. Nev Lavers very kindly said, "I didn't see that," and there was no further mention of the subject. Having passed, I was disappointed at not being able to stay, having been posted to Airlines of South Australia based in Adelaide.

Due to the intensity of my training, I had only managed one trip home to my family and now I was faced with telling them I was off yet again, to another basing. Luckily my parents were living in Adelaide and were only too happy to provide accommodation which certainly helped to lower the stress level.

Airlines of South Australia were an even tighter operation than ANSW, having only four aircraft, three in the local colour scheme and one in the Ansett colours. With the luxury of hindsight, I arrived in Adelaide quietly overconfident, having been cleared to the line and viewed the local check flight a formality. This was very nearly my undoing as this Airline seemed to interpret the manual slightly differently to ANSW. In fact, my procedural flying was so far off the mark, Tony Mooy, the Check Captain, cancelled the check in mid-flight. Instead of failing me, it was re-graded as a progress flight. For some reason, Tony saw fit to give me a go and for this I was grateful.

I quickly got my act together and learned to fly the ASA way, passed the check-out, and enjoyed four months with the airline. The airline flew short sectors to Kingscote on Kangaroo Island, Mt Gambier, Port Lincoln, Ceduna, Whyalla, Port Augusta, Broken Hill and one relatively long sector to Moomba in the far north of the state. Moomba was the site of the gas pipeline and a familiar destination from my charter days. As it was unsealed at the time, I always enjoyed racing down the runway in a giant cloud of yellow dust. The countryside was spectacular with miles of dunes and salt lakes with exotic names like Starvation Lake. At night, the flame from the gas burn-off could be seen a hundred miles away and over the pitch-black desert, it gave the horizon an eerie glow.

The Friendship was by now starting to feel familiar. With a climb speed of 180 knots, a cruise of 240 knots and a descent of 230 knots, it was hardly a rocket but a solidly built and a very stable aircraft. During cruise, the fuel flow was around 1,500 lbs an hour and among the local communities it was known as a trusted and reliable form of transportation. I did, however, feel that airline flying was not what I thought it would be. The local captains were even more insular than the ANSW ones and had little or no idea of the industry outside their little world. It always surprised me when they would ask questions like, "Was the Nomad IFR?" When I replied that they had double the navigation aids of their almighty Fokker, the cockpit would become noticeably quiet.

6.2 *George Palmer and F27 of Airlines of South Australia, VH-FNP, November 1981.*

There was one Irish Captain I enjoyed flying with immensely; for six months his staff identification card had a picture of his dog, aptly named Captain Barker. It was more than an add-on, very professionally done and laminated. He was an ex-helicopter pilot and one of the funniest people I have ever met. Every trip he would have me in stitches, he was a true eccentric.

On one overnight, he parked the aircraft with the wingtip strategically positioned over a deep drain. It was the first officer's duty to put the aircraft to bed which required all the control locks and covers to be in place. "Cleats and covers on and I'll be seeing yer on de bus," he said in his broad Irish accent. This was obviously a set-up with the deep drain preventing me from reaching the ailerons using the pole for the aileron cleats. Once he was out of sight, I rolled an empty 44-gallon drum into the drain, stood it up and climbed on top of it as a ladder. Within minutes I had all the locks and covers on and joined my Irish captain on the bus. "Did you do both ailerons?" he asked. Looking back at the aircraft he could see both red tags fluttering in the breeze. With the fuel drum rolled over and out of sight I could see that he was immediately intrigued on how I did it, but he said nothing, he just raised both eyebrows and gave me a sheepish grin. No-one knew where he lived. He never gave the company an address or home phone number and never socialised outside company business. We did not even know if he was married. After a flight he would walk off through the carpark with a school bag tossed over his shoulder and simply disappear.

I decided it was time to move the family to Adelaide but in the middle of the preparations, I received the news I was now required to transfer to Main-Line in Melbourne. It was still flying the Fokker, but Main-Line was the avenue to the coveted jets. Eight months after joining the company, I was finally able to live with my family and move into the family home.

Melbourne, being the headquarters of the parent company, was a different world to the small subsidiary airlines. Nothing happened quickly, it reminded me of my Air Force days with procedural paperwork and it was over a week before I was checked out. Once again, things were done differently, but again, I was fortunate in having a true gentleman on the check ride. Derek Scherer was an Austrian who had migrated to Australia. Still with a broad Austrian accent, he was kind enough to treat the exercise more as a training detail than a test, especially as this was my third move in less than a year. "Dis is how vee do it here," he would say.

We flew from Melbourne to Hamilton, the home of Ansett, where Reg Ansett, during the thirties began ferrying passengers to Melbourne by car. Due to the surrounding terrain, Hamilton required entry into a NDB let-down and then a visual circuit to the runway, all of which Derek talked me through the correct procedure. We then flew to Mt Gambier, which I was familiar with and then back to Melbourne via Hamilton again. Derek commuted to Brisbane and on landing was keen to catch the last flight out. "Good verk, George, I vill fill out zee paperwork on zee flight home," he yelled as he raced off across the tarmac, overnight bag swinging against his legs. That obviously was the end of the briefing! Sitting quietly in the cockpit on my own, I thought I must now be the most checked-out Fokker pilot in the world.

Melbourne proved to be a different world to the subsidiaries. Main-Line was the big league and I now realised my seniority did not rate a flying block (a flying roster). In fact, it did not rate anything, and 'reserve' was my new status. Week after week went by with only one or two callouts. Often the flights were to act as safety pilot for someone under training and I would simply sit in the jump seat to observe. I found this to be a soul-destroying job. I began to fly only 10 hours a month and worse it became difficult to maintain a standard. When I did fly in a control seat, I started to make stupid mistakes and it all became quite depressing.

Everything comes to he who waits, as they say and finally, after a year in the company, I rated a flying block with a full roster. The flying blocks were advertised a month in advance for both captains and first officers. Numbered as individual rosters, the successful bidders would fly as a team for the complete month. This system proved very enjoyable if you scored a partner whom you got on well with and a complete nightmare if you did not. The captain's blocks were available first and F/Os, if senior enough, could pick and choose with whom they flew. It goes without saying that being the most junior block holder, a vast number of unpleasant scenarios were within the realms of possibility. On my first flying block I was paired up with Geoff Noble who had recently gained his Command. Geoff proved to be a most amicable partner but being a brand-new convert, he was not allowed to give away take-offs and landings. Thus, we had a very enjoyable month together but not once did I touch the controls!

The next month I scored a Supervisors' Roster, flying with a variety of Check Captains which included being the support pilot for two Initial Command check-outs. On one, the captain under check made the mistake of giving a most interesting public address to the passengers over the radio. I sat there for a while, wondering why I could hear this through the headset. By the time the penny dropped and I called, "You are on the air!" it was too late; the airways were full of smart-arse comments from other aircraft. The Check Captain was sitting in the jump-seat behind us. Observing any need to interfere in the flight would result in the check being graded as a fail. The icy look I received made it clear that the late 'pick-up' of the captain's error was noted. Oh, how I wished I were back in my Nomad over the Timor Sea, looking forward to a beer with Gundy.

Somehow, I survived this junior period of being over-exposed, but several pilots did not, and I realised that it was one thing to be admitted to the airlines and another to stay there. Twice a year we had Base-Checks conducted at Avalon, demonstrating our handling of emergency procedures and general flying ability. Once a year, there was a Line-Check to observe a normal operation which could and often did go over two days. Any failure resulted in re-training and if the re-check was unsuccessful, that was it: out the door. On top of this, twice a year, a medical examination had to be passed. Once a modicum of seniority was gained, it seemed the system backed off a little, especially after gaining the second stripe after two years of service. Once I reached this dizzy status, I not only held a flying block, but it was free of encumbrances and I was operating the aircraft on a leg for leg basis.

One of the more enjoyable roster patterns was called The Track Trip; this was in reference to how the locals in Darwin referred to any road travel south towards Alice Springs. Another favourite sequence was the return flights out to Ayers Rock from Alice Springs. The jets also had a version of the Track Trip that commenced out of Melbourne, landed in Adelaide and Alice Springs with a night stopover in Darwin. Two very senior pilots on the 727 used to regularly bid to fly together on this roster, with both sharing the Christian name Jack. They became known as the Two Jacks and were a regular feature of a Darwin layover. Along with the F-27 and 727 crews, an F-28 crew from Perth also spent the night in the hotel. All crews arrived in the early evening and all were not due to sign on again until late the following afternoon. It was a recipe for disaster, especially if the Two Jacks were holding court.

Some of the images etched into my memory are unforgettable, like a fully clothed flight engineer demonstrating his ability to walk on water, only to disappear to the bottom of the hotel pool clutching a raised wine glass. One crew even managed to spend the night in the local lock-up. Frank, the F/O, saw fit to crawl under a table and bite a girl on the leg. The boyfriend, predictably, went berserk and the captain and flight engineer had to come to Frank's rescue. The result was the entire cockpit crew being arrested by the local constabulary and thrown into jail. Spiderman was another wild character who specialised in walking around the Travel Lodge on the outside walls via the tiny balconies several floors up. There was something in the water up there, but we had a marvellous time and somehow survived serious repercussions.

On 1 October 1982, I was awarded a First Officer position on the Boeing 737. This was more like it: after eleven years of professional flying, I was finally going to fly a jet.

7
JETS AT LAST
1982

*Once you have tasted flight, you will forever walk the earth
with your eyes turned skyward, for there you have been,
and there you will always long to return.*

Leonardo da Vinci

The 737-course commenced with a ground school at Melbourne Airports Astro-Jet Centre – a strange place, very cold and sterile. The building housed the company's Operational Management including the Chief Pilot, the individual Fleet Managers and the Flight Safety Department. The long-deserted corridors seemed very intimidating. The walls were covered with portraits of previous management, resplendent in their uniforms, with very humourless expressions, glaring intently into space. Other framed pictures depicted the company's aircraft, invariably with the background of the Sydney Harbour Bridge or Ayers Rock. The floors were highly polished, and the air-conditioning seemed to have only one setting: it was always icy cold. An extremely dangerous place, I thought, and our success or failure had profoundly serious consequence:

pass or go back to the F-27. The threatening atmosphere re-ignited my survival instincts. I was going to make every effort not to come unstuck.

The methodology of the course was something I had never seen before, but it became the standard way of doing things. We were organised into pairs and allocated a computer console to watch the individual topics via VCR tapes. I found it difficult to concentrate at times as the American voice droned on in a monotonous grating fashion. Seemingly the course was designed for direct translation into other languages, and this caused such gems as the 'hydraulic pump in the NOT ON position' rather than saying 'OFF.' I found it irritating, but the good news was that the systems seemed very straightforward and easy to understand, especially compared to the F-27. I think the truth of the matter was that Boeing had a refreshing sense of what a pilot needed to know and what he could do about it. I passed all the exams without difficulty and was pleased to learn we were off to Christchurch in New Zealand for the simulator and aircraft endorsement with Air New Zealand.

We flew First Class on an Air New Zealand 747, as one did during the union halcyon days and checked into the Russley Motel in Christchurch. The back fence of the motel adjoined a farmer's paddock and I awoke the next morning to find a large black and white cow staring in through the window. An unusual start for a flying course, I thought, but somehow very Kiwi.

The simulator programme proved to be quite demanding with sessions even after midnight, referred to as 'back of the clock.' It proved to be a very condensed schedule with little time for consolidation. The early simulators were not as advanced as they are today and had a basic visual display with night vision only and no side windows. I over-controlled initially, especially in roll, flying my first approaches like a man under the influence of a prohibited drug. The secret was to lock the arms into the extended arm rests and to fly strictly by the numbers with as little input as possible. It pains me to recollect my first simulated engine failure; we rolled over onto our back, like a shot crow and crashed back onto the runway, exactly on centreline, which seemed to puzzle the instructor. It was all about technique, and happily I quickly grasped it and completed the sessions successfully.

Other course companions included Rod Trower from my Sydney days and Graham Mobray. Ian Poole completed the rostered quartet, a young and relatively inexperienced pilot. Ian taught me a valuable lesson in judging people. Despite the age and experience level differences, he flew like an expert. I, initially, was guilty of thinking he was too inexperienced to be on the course. Experience counts, but so does natural ability: Ian was a natural and proved it most convincingly.

The time came to fly the real aircraft and I was assigned Captain Ted Prebble. Ted was an easy going Kiwi with a practical approach. As it was dark and raining quite heavily, he completed a standard walk-around very quickly and advised me to have a closer look during daylight with better weather. With no time to absorb the historical significance of it all, we taxied out with the windscreen wipers thumping away and were quickly airborne. The aircraft proved to be easier to fly than the simulator and once I caught up with the speed, I completed the necessary circuits and landings to qualify. The landing speed seemed fast, but the aircraft proved to be stable and highly manoeuvrable, and it flew like a fighter – exhilarating!

After I returned to Melbourne, nobody showed the slightest interest in my new status as the World's latest 737 pilot. I was sent home to await the allocation of a Training Captain. In typical airline indifference to normality, two weeks later, just when I thought they had forgotten about me, I was rostered for my first flight on Christmas Day! It seemed all jet instructors must be called Ted, because my new Fleet Manager was Ted Walters and my new Instructor was to be Ted Moore. Ted number three proved to be a quiet, reserved and softly spoken man, a perfect calming influence, for once again I felt the fear of failure. One of my good friends from General Aviation had recently failed a Jet conversion course with the opposition at TAA and it seemed his career was finished. After having come this far, I just had to pass – failure was not an option.

Christmas morning had me quickly handing out presents to the family and then promptly leaving for the airport. My first training flight was to be a normal revenue service to Hobart and return. Ted proved to be an excellent instructor, but it was still like drinking out of a fire hose, so much to learn and absorb. Ted nominated to fly the first sector to allow me to settle down in the support role and I would fly back. We quickly completed the pre-flight duties and began to push back from the Aerobridge. The cockpit seemed cramped and busy, certainly no bigger than the Fokker and it took me a little while to find a place for the never-ending paperwork, maps, data card and personal bits and pieces. Even my headset cord seemed to snag on something if I tried to move my head and I felt strangely outside my comfort zone. Taxiing out, Ted told me to relax and enjoy it but that was easy for him to say!

During the take-off the acceleration was rapid; at rotate speed, where the nose wheel is first lifted off the runway surface, the nose came up to an incredible 20 degrees of pitch completely blocking any forward view. The only thing in the cockpit window was a brilliant blue sky and not only that we were still accelerating! On completing the After Take-Off checklist and now climbing out with the flaps and slats tucked away, I had the first opportunity to look outside. Down below me and rapidly sliding to the rear was Phillip Island. It was quite a jolt to the senses to be this far south already. Lesson number one about flying jets, they wait for no-one!

My first sector as operating pilot went well. I remember that I managed a good approach and landing but not much else and over all I found the 737 an easier conversion process compared with the F-27. The speed, or more accurately, the management of the speed seemed to be the new challenge.

The initial difficulty managing the speed seemed to be the last 30 miles – you judged the descent profile using a basic three-times-your-height formulae for the distance to run plus variations. On top of this the aircraft needed about ten miles to slow down to initial flap selection speed. All this had to fit into Air Traffic Control procedures, not to mention changes in wind speeds or direction. There was a real art to this, and an experienced pilot could make it look easy. In fact, it would look like he was just sitting there watching the world go by. In reality, he was mentally monitoring all the parameters and adjusting accordingly. Like most things, it took time to acquire the mental picture.

At the time, Australia had not adopted the international rule of no more than 250 knots below 10,000 feet, and we would descend at 300 knots to 5,000 feet. This made things happen quickly and mistakes difficult to fix. For some unknown reason, I could readily adjust to this way of thinking. Despite being inept at anything mathematical, I made good progress.

I loved the 737, but on reflection, the early models were a little too light on the controls, especially in roll. Flying a close, low weather circuit at night, trying to judge the turning radius, distance out and so on, it was quite easy to apply excessive bank angles. The aeroplane was also sensitive in pitch and had to be flown accurately at the correct pitch attitude for each configuration. The under-slung engines produced a powerful pitch up with any increase in thrust and conversely a nose drop with any reduction. Speed brakes were available, where, by raising a lever, panels on the upper wing surface would stand up into the airflow and act as aerodynamic drag. It was, however, a matter of pride not to use them and in any case never to use them more than once. Of course, you could use them any time you liked but it did make a glaring announcement to all and sundry, creating a low rumble through the airframe. As co-pilots we often sneeringly referred to them as 'captain's correction levers' and tried hard to judge a profile without using them.

7.1 Ansett Boeing 737 200. Photo taken by Rob Finlayson.

Over a two-month period I completed 40 sectors and passed my check to the line which consisted of five sectors over two days – a sector is one take-off to one landing on the same flight. As before on the F-27, my new status was Reserve and I flew on average only 35 hours a month. The company ran an open-time book advertising any additional flying resulting from sickness, charters or the sad case of somebody failing a check and thus making their flying available. I managed, on average, an extra trip a month. Some senior pilots bid for Reserve in order to run their hobby farms or whatever. I once flew with a captain who operated a restaurant in North Carlton; he loved to boast that he would only fly once a month to stay current. As a flying enthusiast, I had trouble getting my head around this and wondered why they bothered to turn up at all. The answer, of course, was they could benefit greatly from two incomes. This perk was doomed to fall over dramatically in a few years, as events would prove.

The early 737-200 was powered by Pratt and Whitney JT-8-15 engines producing 15,500 lbs of thrust and by today's standards they were thirsty, noisy engines. The thrust reversers consisted of two clam shell doors, operated hydraulically, that swung out to cover the tailpipe. This resulted in the thrust being deflected forward and was often referred to as a Hot Reverser. On completing the walk-around inspection, I always quickened my step to avoid them, as I had a fear they would suddenly pop out and cut me in half. On take-off, the engines emitted a very satisfying 'crackle', sounding like somebody tearing a sheet of cardboard at high speed. If you were standing near the runway, you could feel the ground vibrate. It was a wonderful sound and was soon to come under the scrutiny of the anti-noise crowd, those strange folks who build their houses alongside an airport and suddenly discover that aeroplanes use airports. People would build next to a railway-line and have trains thundering past their back fence and never say a word, but the mere sight of an aircraft would have them waving their placards in furious indignation of it all.

The local aviation media hailed the aircraft as the first computerised jet in Australia which was slightly wishful thinking. Performance charts were replaced by a Performance Data Computer System or PDCS which could only be considered a considerably basic computer, if that. To extract data, basic parameters had to be first entered which included the aircraft's weight, fuel load and air temperature. Using a rotating selector, optimum cruise altitudes and other performance data could be obtained. Navigation was made easier by a very low frequency navigation aid called VLF Omega. This was a back-up to conventional ground aids, but it too had its limitations. Sometimes during heavy rain, it would simply drop out. We were told by the men in white coats that this was due to the 'H' type field antenna. Nobody of course would admit they did not know what an 'H' type antenna was.

One of the more amusing incidents was when the Department of Transport, aware of this problem, insisted on two Omegas for long ocean crossings. Ansett at the time was conducting flights on behalf of Polynesian Airlines in the Pacific. One aircraft to be used on this contract was subsequently fitted with two Omega units. When faced with heavy rain for the first time and much to the amusement of the line crews, both promptly failed. You could have had ten of the bloody things for all the difference it made.

I quickly settled into a routine and tried hard to be a good co-pilot. These were the days before Cockpit Resource Management, HR departments and other programmes, which are common today. Cockpit Resource Management was introduced in the late seventies after several bad accidents attributed to pilot error, or more accurately, human failings in communication and teamwork. Most of the captains were a pleasure to work with but we had our fair share of complete tyrants and the odd individual who, politely, could only be called 'different'. One, we called Captain Late; no matter what the task, he had to be 'late.' He would not only sign on late, but he would also sign off late – holding up the crew bus for an overnight hotel was a speciality. Another captain was called The Astronaut because no matter what the wind direction, he would always go as high as physically possible.

At high altitudes, the stall speed at the low end of the speed scale and the Mach high speed buffet, caused by the shock wave starting to move aft in the thin air, would gradually come together. At high altitude, the air is less dense or thinner. To achieve sufficient lift, the wing has to fly at a higher angle of attack. The angle of attack is the angle of the wing to the relative airflow. The angle of attack that creates the most lift is called the critical angle of attack. Any increase past this angle, the smooth laminar flow over the wing begins to break down or separate. This then is the cause of a rapid loss in lift or a stall.

The high-speed argument is also interesting. The higher you fly the colder the air (until the tropopause), with the temperature falling by two degrees per each thousand feet. The air is a gas and gas molecules move more slowly in colder air than they do in warmer temperatures. As a result, the speed of sound is reached at a lower speed than at sea level. As the airflow reaches supersonic speed, a shock wave begins to form which will also begin an airflow separation.

In reality this is a brief description of a complex aerodynamic condition, but it is safe to say that as you fly higher the stall speed and the critical Mach number slowly move towards each other. All Boeings have a stick shaker as a warning of the slow speed limit; the control column literally shakes in its mounts. The high-speed warning is an audio clacking, commonly called the cricket because that what it sounds like. Reaching this altitude where these two limits begin to merge is known as coffin corner. This is eventually the limit to any aircraft's maximum altitude capability or what is termed the service ceiling. It is easy to lose a few knots in unstable air, especially in turbulence associated with high level cloud. Prudent pilots would give themselves a healthy split between high and low speed buffet limits. Flying at the absolute maximum all the time lowered these margins to a fine degree and it seemed pointless to me, if not the optimum altitude for economy. There were, of course, many captains who were great to fly with and a few became lifelong friends. Somehow, I learnt to work and live with these characters and kept my nose clean, but it was not easy.

Once, taking off from Hobart with the captain conducting the take-off, we hit a hare. The bounding animal left its run into the grass a little late. With the cockpit sitting right over the nose wheel there was a distinct thump as the poor creature met its end at about 140 knots. On landing in Melbourne, we both went down on to the tarmac to see if we had inflicted any damage. I was surprised to see considerable blood and fur all over the nose wheel and taxi light.

The engineers suggested we lodge an Incident Report commonly known as a Form 225. My partner in crime lodged the report as a Mid-Hare collision. Sadly, the Department of Transport and the Safety Manager failed to see the joke and I remember being told that the company was not a home for delinquent schoolboys or something along those lines.

One thing that did require some adjustment was the exposure to licence renewals in a simulator. Twice a year we had Revision or Recurrent Training and twice a year an actual test. Even though the recurrent was officially 'training', if any difficulties were encountered, a repeat would be rostered. So, all simulator sessions had to be treated as an examination. The result was a simulator session every three months. These sessions were of four hours' duration with up to an hour each side for a brief and de-briefing. Some lived in absolute fear of the 'Sim', some loved the challenge and others like me, were somewhere in between. When things were going well, I enjoyed it, but if you were having an off day, the sim could be a stressful experience.

The simulators looked like machines from the movie *Star Wars*, large rectangular boxes sitting on tall hydraulic struts. They were sophisticated and expensive, and had to be kept in a controlled environment. The buildings housing the simulators were always cold. In the background, the air was filled with a deep humming sound; one was reminded of the lower deck noise of a large ship. The air even had its own smell, an odd metallic mixture of cold steel and hospital disinfectant. Hard to describe but with my eyes shut that smell would instantly tell me where I was.

Some pilots called it the Bat Cave, the Lurching Cave or simply the Box. Failure to demonstrate the required standard inevitably led to re-training or dismissal. A subtle pressure on all airline pilots to perform, which some handled better than others. The simulator could be a wonderful training aid, but financial pressures, time constraints and an endless regulatory renewal programme often meant this was a lost opportunity. It was also a place where egos could run riot. The senior boys of a boarding school would love a simulator to harass and torture the first-year boarders. Grown men were driven to tears and careers could be torn up in a heartbeat. For egotistical megalomaniacs, a simulator was pure heaven.

Something new in flying jets was a new perspective of the sky. On some trips we never saw the ground throughout the entire flight. The view was replaced by magnificent landscapes of towering clouds or wafer-thin layers of transparent cirrus that would flash past in a heartbeat… or grey brooding stratus in a solid flat overcast stretching from horizon to horizon. Rainbows in a complete circle with a shadow of the aircraft dead centre would race along beside the wingtip only to disappear just as quickly as they came. Red rays of light pouring out from behind the cloud tops, with the cloud edges a brilliant gold. Sunrises and sunsets of incredible beauty would turn the whole sky red and orange. Giant brooding, evil-looking thunderstorms, impossible to describe in their sheer beauty and power, would flash and light up the sky like some maniacal electric short circuit. Above 40,000 feet the natural horizon would bend at the edges and the top of the sky would be a deep royal blue, magnificent, vast and somehow intimidating. Contrails would appear jet-black or snow-white, depending on the backlight. Other aeroplanes looked like tiny insects trailing through the sky. I always found it difficult to visualise that inside these insects were people sleeping, reading or having lobster in First Class. Against this visual spectacle of nature, humans and their machines looked ridiculously inadequate.

One thing that always puzzled me – a quick glance at the cabin on my way to the washroom would show all the passengers sitting there with their shades down, ignoring this mind-numbing view of nature. Had they seen it all before? Are these the same people who spend hours driving into the hills on a weekend to take photographs of the view from the marked lookouts? Here we were at 37,000 feet with a horizon of a hundred miles, a view to die for and nobody is remotely interested!

I gradually settled into a steady lifestyle and gained enough seniority to guarantee a normal flying roster. For the first time in my career, I had a steady job with a good income. However, all was not well on the home front and after many unhappy years, I finally split up with my wife for good. I moved into a flat in North Fitzroy along with all my aviation memorabilia, model aeroplanes and books. The parting words of my wife perhaps summed up my situation rather succinctly, "If you had a proper job, we might have worked," she said. Access to my daughter proved difficult with roster changes constantly interfering with the nominated days of access. Maybe she was right; I did not have a 'proper job' but I would not change it for the world.

8
POLYNESIAN AIRLINES
1985

Don't worry, we leave on Samoa time.
Despatcher Polynesian Airlines, September 1985

In August 1985, Alf Gloster rang me at home and asked if I was interested in going to Polynesian Airlines. They needed Nomad pilots for a short contract of three months. Knowing I was ex-Nomad, together with former Connair pilot Geoff Austin, he considered us a natural choice. The position was unaccompanied, and not only did I have my daughter to think off, but I had met a lovely girl and seemed on the brink of a new relationship. I agreed to a short-term contract and within days was packing my bags to move to Apia in Western Samoa.

Prior to leaving Australia, I attended an interview with Bill Hanrahan, Head of Flight Operations at the time. I was reminded that I was representing the company and any adverse feedback would be viewed negatively and be detrimental to my future! Having assured the boss I would uphold the fine reputation of Ansett, I had cause to remember this interview with some amusement. On my first familiarisation flight into Pago Pago, I was surprised to hear the local operator call the tower, with a Texan drawl, "Howdy Pago Tower, this is Pacific 25 coming down the big slide for runway 5." Ansett's reputation was looking secure.

Western Samoa consisted basically of two main islands: Upolu and Savaii. The islands were volcanic with Savaii dominated by a large volcano on its eastern edge. Black lava beds protruded into jade-green waters, the contrast producing a scene of incredible beauty. Where sandy beaches existed, the sand was a postcard white, framed by tall coconut trees all leaning towards the sea.

The famous author of the book *Treasure Island*, Robert Louis Stevenson, was buried below the summit of Mount Vaea, Upolu behind the Hotel Tusitala. Tusitala is translated as Teller of Tales. Stevenson died 3 December 1894 at the young age of 44.

Together with the Nomad, I flew a Britten-Norman Islander (BN-2), an English designed light twin with a high wing and fixed undercarriage. As it was rugged and versatile, I enjoyed the aircraft immensely, but it was very noisy. It always felt like working in a sawmill. Living in a holiday-style cabin, I enjoyed the flying and after-hours had a very agreeable social life. One of the crewing officers played in the local band so the nightly dance became the kick-off point for a long and entertaining evening. By today's standards we probably drank too much, and propeller blades howling beside your head the following morning were not conducive to a quick recovery!

We flew to three local airports and across to American Samoa to Pago Pago. Approaching Pago for the first time via an Instrument Landing Approach on Runway 05, I was interested to see a small hill just shy of the threshold. On top of this hill was a long trench-like scar, a left-over mark from another aviation tragedy. A Pan Am Boeing 707 undershot the runway, took the top off the hill, finally rolling to a stop on the runway edge. All on board were killed, and this was another reminder of 'getting it wrong' and the consequences of doing so.

While the schedule with Polynesian was fixed, the locals had that very relaxed sense of urgency common among the Pacific islands. Trying to run on time would produce puzzled looks and comments about Samoa Time. I found this frustrating at first but once I accepted this was the way it worked, I relaxed into their style, a wonderful 'be happy, don't worry' attitude that quickly became infectious.

The Samoan scenery was stunningly beautiful, and I once saw the main volcano on Savaii Island was clear of cloud, an exceedingly rare event. Being alone in the Islander, VFR and inbound to the coastal town of Asau, I decided to investigate and climbed rapidly towards the summit. Approaching the lip, I had the idea of looking inside the crater itself. Just as I was about to cross the jagged edge, I ran into turbulence that was extremely violent and completely lost control of the aircraft to the point I was literally flung down the far side of the slope. Taking nature's hint, I quietly retreated and descended towards Asau. I have often wondered since, if I had been pushed into the crater and run into more turbulence would I have been able to get out again? On the return trip, the summit was buried in thick cloud.

After two months I began to miss my daughter and Melissa, my new girlfriend. I ran up a mammoth phone bill ringing home to the point the local telephonist knew me personally. Eventually the contract came to an end and I returned to Australia. Melissa and I became engaged, and I resumed my duties as a co-pilot on the 737.

As a side note, my replacement pilot subsequently destroyed the venerable BN-2 Islander by overrunning the strip at Asau. The strip was bounded at both ends by the sea and the aircraft went off one end, quickly sinking into oblivion in deep water. Fortunately, apart from a lesson in underwater swimming, our pilot, the only occupant, was unharmed. To add insult to injury the following year the volcano erupted, the pyroclastic flow of lava rolling right over the strip and nearby waterfront which now no longer exists.

A more comprehensive method of destroying the evidence is hard to imagine.

8.1 Ansett Air Freight Boeing 727 200F. Photo taken by Rob Finlayson.

I had my own water experience during my Samoan contract, nearly drowning despite being considered a strong swimmer. I had sought and gained permission from a village elder to swim off the local beach. This was a requirement as the village had full control of beach access. I was only a few metres from the shore in deep but crystal-clear water when the water temperature suddenly dropped. For some strange reason, I glanced at the sea floor and noticed the sand and general debris rolling rapidly along like tumbleweeds in a wind. I broke to the surface only to find the beach moving away like a movie being played backwards. I was in a rip and what is more, it was an extremely powerful one.

I remembered the golden rule of swimming parallel to the beach, but it still looked like I was going to end up in Los Angeles. Finally, the water became warm again and I was free but totally exhausted.

Too exhausted to swim back to the beach, I floated around on my back for twenty minutes finally regaining enough strength to make it to the beach. I discovered later that an underground freshwater spring would sometimes penetrate the seafloor. I suggested to the locals that a warning sign would be a good idea, but they just responded with that 'don't worry, be happy' look.

The transfer to Polynesian Airlines was a highlight of my Ansett career. This favourable experience would save my career when in the future I volunteered to go to Singapore Airlines.

On returning to Ansett, I completed a refresher in the simulator and was quickly absorbed back into the system. I was averaging only six nights away a month and flying anything from one sector to three a day, a very pleasant pace.

The following year after my return from Polynesia, I was on a Sydney overnight and watching the news in my room. To my horror I heard Bill Surh mentioned in relation to an Air Ambulance accident. It quickly became obvious that my old mentor was dead. Taking off from Essendon in Victoria with a nurse and four patients as passengers, Bill lost the left engine on his twin-engine Cessna 402. Climbing slowly to the north of the field, Bill was confronted with the massive power cables that transverse the Tullamarine Freeway. In trying to avoid them he got below VMCA speed and lost control. They never stood a chance as the aircraft exploded into a ball of fire. It was like losing a parent to me. Bill was a major supporter in my early days, and I owed him a lot. For many years I would fly over that spot and silently salute Dr Bill Surh, the flying dentist.

Melissa, or Liss as I always called her, lived in a unit in North Adelaide overlooking a park opposite the Adelaide Zoo. It was not unusual to wake up in the morning to all sorts of strange noises, especially the hooting from a pair of orangutans. I eventually moved in and began to commute from Melbourne. Bidding for Adelaide overnights gave some relief but even then, I spent on average seven nights a month in Melbourne.

I moved into a halfway house in Melbourne, shared by six other commuters, one other Adelaide-domiciled pilot but the others from Brisbane and Sydney. I offered my car as community transport with the proviso it was always available for my visits. Then if I had a layover, one of the other pilots would pick me up from the airport. On one occasion, the police pulled the car over due to a faulty brake light. On questioning the two pilots in the car, they explained that the car belonged to me who lived in Adelaide, the driver had a NSW licence and lived in Sydney, the passenger lived in Queensland and the car was still registered in Victoria to my old address, as the one in the system. The policeman slowly closed his note pad and said, "For Christ's sake, will you just go away," and as an afterthought, "Fix that brake light!" Not living a normal life did have its advantages after all.

I was now established in a new relationship, rated a good choice of flying with a higher seniority number and my efforts in the simulator and line checks were showing good results. The next few years contain many fond memories flying throughout Australia and even trips to Vanuatu and Samoa. Liss and I were married; the only disappointment was that the Church of England refused us a marriage ceremony in a church because I had been married before. I still hold a deep resentment over this decision, and I have not attended a church service since. Liss always wanted to be married in her school chapel and was deeply disappointed. We were eventually married by a celebrant in a converted church used as a restaurant. During the service, a severe storm rained hailstones on the tin roof making the vows impossible to hear. Tablecloths were used to stop water flooding in under the entrance door and the carpark flooded. Maybe God is indeed C of E but we were happy, even without His blessing and remain so to this day.

After eight years as a first officer, my seniority number was creeping up the line to the coveted 'Command' – at this stage only on a Fokker F-50, an updated and re-engined F-27 Friendship.

A successful bid also meant a move to Sydney. Overshadowing this rise on the Seniority List was the threat of deregulation. For years, the Two Airline Policy had allowed the two main domestic operators sole rights to the major trunk routes. East-West Airlines of Tamworth were also flying RPT routes but was somewhat restricted to country towns. Deregulation not only promised real competition but threatened the wages and conditions of the existing duopoly. The union decided to get in early and hit the companies not only for a pay rise but guarantees to our existing contracts. The companies' views, not unexpectedly, looked at it as an opportunity to extract concessions from the pilot group. A clash of interests was inevitable, but I do not think anybody at the time expected the disastrous outcome.

The domestic pilots were represented by the AFAP (Australian Federation of Airline Pilots) where the international pilots had their own union, and the AIPA (Australian International Pilots Association). The AFAP also represented most of the general aviation pilots. For the domestic pilots, union membership was compulsory with subscriptions deducted automatically from a pilot's pay. During the late eighties, I had become involved in the union magazine *Air Pilot*, and became the assistant editor, writing a few articles and drawing some cartoons. I enjoyed this work but hardly considered myself a 'union man.' Engagement between the company and the pilot group was at an all-time low and it seemed a dispute was now inevitable.

9
PILOTS' DISPUTE
1989

"It's a different game this time, boys. You go out and it's war."
Australian Prime Minister Bob Hawke, 21 August 1989

The AFAP lodged a claim against the domestic airlines for a pay rise of 26 per cent. This was naturally rejected and received much ridicule in the press, but many forgot that this was an ambit claim and a starting point for further negotiations. The damage was done, and it set the stage for a massive backlash against the pilot group.

The dispute started off innocently enough; with both sides issuing bulletins and notices of meetings, it quickly became apparent that a street fight was brewing. Being domiciled in Adelaide, I managed to stay out of the limelight and watched with interest as the pilots voted for a nine-to-five campaign and began to refuse to work outside of these hours. The company replied with all guns blazing and began to issue writs to the unfortunate pilots so rostered.

The final result was a call for a mass meeting at the Coburg Town Hall in Melbourne. I drove over from Adelaide and attended the meeting, only to discover we had all 'resigned.' This was a shock and, in my opinion, a grave error of judgement from the union. Kept at arm's length from all the 'barbeques' by being in Adelaide, I was amazed at the solidarity and the lack of anybody questioning these life-changing decisions by a select few. The Coburg Town Hall meeting on 23 August felt more like a Nuremberg Rally than a meeting of Australian professional pilots. The speakers received standing ovations, stamping feet and loud cheering. I drove the long distance back to Adelaide in a state of disbelief, to be met by a distraught wife who stood at the doorway holding the newspaper headlines. I was now officially unemployed.

With the Samoan secondment I had kept current my Command Instrument Rating (we had Command and co-pilot ratings in those days) and was also current with flying light-twins. I managed to quickly obtain some casual work flying Cessna 402s from Adelaide to Alice Springs on night freight operations. I also flew a few charters to Melbourne where I taxied past all the parked Ansett aircraft, a very sobering experience.

The dispute dragged on and became very ugly, especially after a few pilots began to trickle back to work. Much has been written on this subject and the bitterness from both sides remains to this day. I decided with a few others to return to my job in the first week of November. The repercussions were swift and vicious, death threats, constant late-night calls only to hang up on being answered. The windows on my car in the staff carpark were all smashed except for the windscreen. I even had dog poo delivered in an envelope, which made me laugh – it appealed to my sense of humour for some weird reason. All this intimidation was designed to force a change of mind but for me it had the opposite effect.

After a brief sim check in Melbourne, I arrived for my first flight back with Keith Wallace, to fly a revalidation flight, initially Melbourne to Canberra. Union officials and members on 'scab patrols' were at the terminal taking pictures and noting names of pilots crossing the picket line. The story was that you were not guilty until you 'rolled a wheel.' After completing the pre-start checklist, Keith and I noticed all these miscreants with their noses pressed against the terminal window watching our every move. On being given a 'push-back clearance' from the Apron Controller, Keith released the brakes and looked over towards me. "You are fucked now, Georgie," he said very softly.

So began my post-dispute life. I have mixed feelings, regrets at losing life-long friendships, even feelings of anger towards the principal proponents. I have no regrets whatsoever for going back to my job. The self-destructive nature of the campaign was totally pointless, bordering on stupidity. In my opinion, the status of the airline pilot in the public eye in Australia has never recovered from this sad event.

After being cleared back to line, I was asked by the company if I would act as a Safety Pilot for the various foreign operators that were bought in by the Labor Government to break the dispute. The approvals for these operators were only for the principal inter-city pairings. For flights to Cairns and Townsville, for example, an Australian licensed pilot was required to be in the cockpit. I quickly found myself flying with the Yugoslavs of JAT Airlines, the English from the company Paramount and the Americans from Air West. My job was to keep them abreast of all local procedures and to make sure they conformed to Australian rules and regulations. To say this was interesting is an understatement.

I was well familiar with the 737 by this stage and the various methods of completing the same job were fascinating. The Yugoslavs were probably the closest aligned to the Ansett way of doing things, but the captains had an extremely poor grasp of English. The younger co-pilots were better, which made communication bearable. The Americans, on the other hand, seemed overly casual to me, but in fairness, they flew well and were very pleasant characters to share a beer with. The Americans' radio style was more akin to talking to their best pal on the telephone and their briefings were, to say the least, different. They came up with some real classics which kept me amused for days. One take-off briefing went: "Okay, guys, if we lose a stove and find ourselves down in the weeds we will clean up over the sea and return for a visual." Yes, quite. The English pilots of Paramount were equally pleasant company but completely overloaded the poor co-pilot, using him in a slave-like relationship, where he seemed to do everything. With the emphasis within the airline industry of Crew Resource Management, I found this experience invaluable and learned some better ways of doing things.

After two months I was called into Head Office for a Command Interview. Knowing I was close to a Fokker Command prior to the dispute, I frantically studied up on my old Fokker notes only to be offered a slot on the Boeing 727! I asked if it was possible to just change seats on the 737 but Alf Gloster, the Manager of Flight Operations, was adamant that the 727 was the offer. "It will be better for your career," he said. I left feeling a little overwhelmed; I had never flown 'three crew' before, as the 727 flight-deck included a flight engineer, and felt I had some work ahead of me.

10
INITIAL COMMAND
1990

*"Important things are ability and knowledge,
but the biggest decision is, would I let my family
fly with you?"*

Bruce Dewar, B727 Fleet Manager Ansett Airlines, 1990

The Boeing 727 was a real pilot's aeroplane. At the time of my assignment, Ansett had two principal variants, the 200 and the 200LR. The B727-200LR was a version designed for Ansett to enable flights direct from Sydney to Perth, a flight of some five hours. To achieve this, the 'LR' version (for Long Range) had an extra forward auxiliary tank containing 5,400 lbs of useable fuel. The airframe was also beefed up to enable higher operating weights: a maximum take-off weight of 89,358kg as against 86,409kg for the standard 200 series. The landing weights for both versions remained the same. The Ansett aircraft were also fitted with nose wheel brakes and both had the same engines, the Pratt and Whitney JT-8-15s with 15,500 lbs of thrust each. The aircraft had a similar navigation fit to the 737 and utilised the PDCS and VLF Omega systems.

The big difference for me was working with a flight engineer. In Australia, unlike some countries, the flight engineers were not pilots but professional engineers. Some had literally completed their apprenticeships on the 727, followed by years on the shop floor maintaining them before transiting to the cockpit. Many did have pilot licences, varying from Private to Commercial. With all this background they tended to be older than the pilots and known by all to be a no-nonsense group and to call a spade a shovel.

The usual course procedure began almost immediately, with four weeks of ground school followed by four weeks of gruelling simulator work. Far from finding the engineers intimidating, I discovered them to be invaluable in support and encouragement and were an excellent bunch of people. I passed all this initial stage and due to the fact the 727 simulator was not certified for landing credits, I was rostered with three others for a session of circuits at Avalon near Geelong.

Avalon always seemed to me to be an airport in the middle of nowhere. With strong westerly winds the norm, some genius from the past had built the runway aligned north/south, so, there was always a crosswind. The Fleet Manager of the 727, Captain Bruce Dewar, had a reputation of not suffering fools and was nicknamed the Blue Heeler after Australia's famous breed of cattle dog. It was said, if he found a weakness he would bite and not let go!

The aircraft also suffered from a reputation of being difficult to land, especially with full flap of 40 degrees. Armed with all this scuttlebutt and knowing the wind was gusting 15 knots across the strip, we taxied out in Melbourne in a silent cockpit devoid of small talk. Like going to a bloody funeral, I thought at the time.

The first candidate was an American pilot who had joined us during the recent industrial dispute. He flew the aircraft well enough, but his landings were terrible. Sitting in the jump-seat I had the advantage of analysing what was going wrong. It seemed to me he was not stable enough and not controlling the sink, especially during the flare where I thought he was pulling the power off too early.

After the last landing dropped all the oxygen masks, Bruce said nothing. Turning to me, he said quietly through clenched teeth, "Do you want to show me that you can do better than that?" I strapped into the left seat and tried to appear as calm as possible, but inside, I was one notch off having a nervous breakdown! This was the big one, the command upgrade endorsement!

I took off and flew what I thought was a tight circuit and Bruce made some caustic comment about being on a cross-country. The engineer read out the checklist in a strained voice and prepared to end his days with my first attempt at landing. The aeroplane was a delight to fly but had a high wing loading, was prone to sinking out during the flare and was very unforgiving if you ended up slow with a high descent rate. I kept the power on during the flare, closed the thrust levers very slowly and just released any back pressure with no attempt to hold it off. It touched down firmer than I thought it should but much gentler than my American companion. "Piece of cake," growled Bruce and my confidence was restored! After a few more circuits I pulled off a smooth landing (referred to as a greaser in the trade) and Bruce was happy to swap back to the first candidate.

The American still did not get it right and was scrubbed after we returned to Melbourne. I felt so sorry for him, until much later it turned out his experience was not quite what he claimed it to be when he joined us. He quickly disappeared from the company a month later after the Flight Department made a few enquiries into his history.

My Line Training commenced quickly, the first flight was on 26 August 1990. The logbook records a flight from Melbourne to Brisbane, down to Sydney, back up to Brisbane and then returning to Sydney for an overnight. This became a typical pairing of what the crews referred to as the Shark Patrol, that is, up and down the East Coast. Compared to the 737, the 727 was a beautiful aircraft to fly, fast and exceptionally stable in pitch with any power changes. It reminded me of when Hanna Reitsch, the famous female German test pilot of World War II, was asked her impression of her first flight in the rocket powered Me163, she said; "It was like sitting on a cannonball, unbelievable!" The 727 felt like that, a real thoroughbred racehorse.

10.1 Ansett Boeing 727 200. Photo taken by Rob Finlayson.

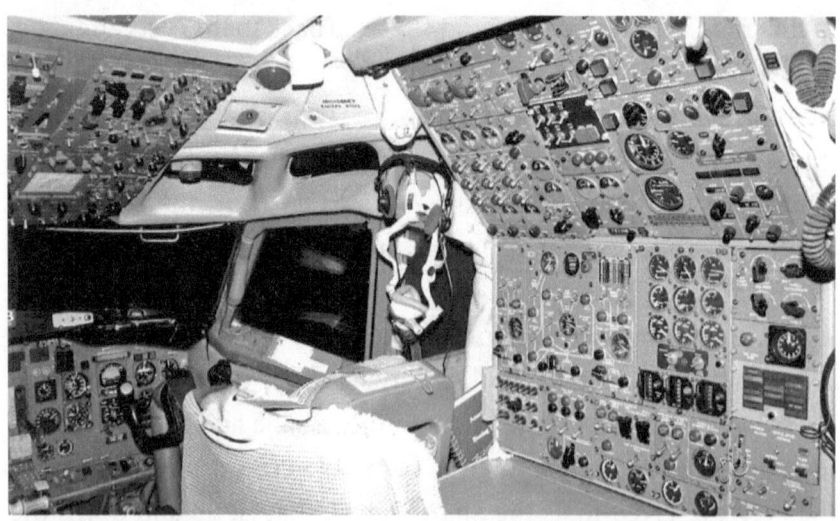

10.2 Flight Engineer's panel Ansett Boeing 727-200 LR, 1990.

The runway performance on a hot day was sluggish, almost as if it were reluctant to get airborne. Once up and accelerating it climbed at speeds of up to 350 knots indicated. No sound at all could be heard from the engines, the only noise a hissing of air around the cockpit windows. The poor unfortunate passengers in the last back row could hear the engines alright, with a pulsating whine, but up front, it was the quietest cockpit I have ever experienced. A favourite trick was to temporarily level off over a flat layer of cloud and accelerate to maximum speed. The sensation was intoxicating as ridges and lumps of cloud flashed past the cockpit windows. A few seconds of madness and then a gentle pull-back into a climb with the 'cloud-floor' dropping away like a stone. The 727 handled turbulence much better than the 737, just giving an irritable shake where you would then hear the forward galley containers rattling away against their locks. The 737 on the other hand, would wallow and roll about and was not nearly as stable.

My training progressed satisfactorily, although every now and then a landing would be a 'thumper' for inexplicable reasons. It took me a while to understand that to get a 'greaser' you just had to kill off any sink, be speed stable and not take the power off too quickly. It had the long-term effect of making my flying smoother, but it would still bite without mercy if you relaxed the concentration. After one firm landing in Canberra, one of the flight attendants came in and placed a glass of water on the console and said, "Georgie dearest, if you are going to plant it, you had better water it!" My training captain thought this was hilarious, but I did not. Aviation can be very humbling at times.

After two months of flying the line with a training captain, I was deemed ready for the Progress Check, which apart from checking the new candidate's progress was the issue of the First-Class Airline Transport Pilots Licence. Co-pilots at the time operated on a Second-Class Licence. (Today the Second-Class ATPL Licence no longer exists, some co-pilots even flying on a Commercial Licence).

I was rostered to fly with John Dorward who was the Director of Flight Operations (DFO), or just 'God' to a trainee captain.

The first sector was Sydney to Brisbane and on the approach, the landing gear failed to show that it was down and locked correctly. Instead of asking the flight engineer, John directed me to go down the back and check the Main Gear Viewer. Five feet behind the last window exit on the left-hand side was a circular patch in the carpet which was held down with Velcro. On lifting this up, it was possible to remove a cover exposing a glass mirror where a visual inspection of the offending undercarriage could be carried out. Looking through the mirror two red indices could be checked for correct alignment.

Two unfortunate set of circumstances were quickly apparent. Firstly, the flight was full, and the seat belt sign was on and secondly, a young lady was sitting in the seat overhanging the carpet section containing the cover. To add to my predicament, she was wearing a noticeably short mini skirt. Much to the amusement of the surrounding passengers, let alone the audible giggling of an adjacent flight attendant, I was forced to kneel at the feet of the young lass on all fours and go about my technical business! She very kindly held the removed floor cover strategically in front of her knees. The undercarriage quickly proved itself to be 'down and locked' and apparently with a complexion the colour of bright red, I retreated to the cockpit. Both John and the flight engineer were highly amused on hearing the details from the laughing cabin crew. It did have the effect of lowering the tension level of it being a Check Flight and the rest of the check was without incident.

Even though I now held a First-Class Licence, I still had to pass the final checkout (Check to the Line or CTL). The CTL is the final test before being released into the system. Before the CTL I had to pass a Flight Proficiency Check. I was rostered with the Blue Heeler again at Avalon, doing among other things, asymmetric circuits and bad weather circuits. I remember quite clearly watching the local farmers' sheep scattering like cockroaches after a light was turned on. We thundered over their heads at 400 feet, tearing the air apart. All went well and now all I had to do was finish the required sectors with my training captain and pass the final CTL.

23 October proved to be the big day, well, in reality, the first day, as the CTL was programmed over two days. The first day the Check Captain flew in the right seat and acted as a co-pilot while the real co-pilot sat in the observer's seat (referred to as a jump-seat). Passing the first day, the examiner would swap places with the co-pilot and just observe from the jump-seat. At this stage, any interference or action deemed necessary from the Check Captain would be marked instantly as a fail. The first day was scheduled out of Melbourne to Sydney, on to Hamilton Island, back to Sydney and Melbourne. The second day was to fly as a passenger to Sydney and then crew from Sydney to Canberra, back to Sydney and finally home to Melbourne. The rostered Check Captain was Bruce Dewar, the Blue Heeler.

I arrived early, complete with a fresh haircut, immaculate uniform and spit-polished shoes only to be confronted with an awful weather forecast. Hamilton Island was going to be the problem as there was no precision approach available and the forecast was for low cloud with passing rain showers. The first leg to Sydney went well and I seemed to get most of Bruce's questions correct.

After a quick turn-around we departed for Hamilton Island and sure enough, the weather was terrible with rain showers and a strong southerly. This required a non-precision approach to Runway 32 and then a low-level circling approach to land into wind on the opposite end, Runway 14. I could tell by Bruce sliding his seat forward and the noticeable tension in the flight engineer's voice that this was going to be show time. The approach went well enough and we broke out of the cloud base and turned left to join for a low downwind for runway 14. At this stage, the rain became heavier, but I considered I was still visual and flew around Dent Island, a narrow rocky island just off the centreline. With all checks completed the rest of the approach went well and with the windscreen wipers clanking away, we touched down smoothly on the correct spot. After taxiing into the small apron, which was surrounded by an old quarry, we shut down.

At this stage nothing had been said and the cockpit was eerily silent. "What can you tell me about the rules for a low weather circling approach, Captain?" Bruce snarled and seemed to emphasise the word 'Captain'. I rattled off all the rules and regulations and Bruce said, "What about the fact that you must have the runway in sight at all times?' he growled back. "When you went behind Dent Island, I couldn't even see the bloody airfield let alone the runway." I replied that Dent Island was a 'feature' of the runway environment and that was acceptable. He muttered, "I see," and stomped off towards the terminal. I found out later he made a phone call.

Both the co-pilot and the engineer started saying how sorry they were, and they thought I had blown it. I was convinced I was right, but I began to get a real sinking feeling in the pit of my stomach. Bruce came back into the cockpit and you could have heard a pin drop. "You are quite right, George; I have never thought about this scenario here before. There is no way you can turn inside Dent Island." The relief flooded through me like a wave. "Carry on, Captain," he snapped, and I very nearly gave him an "Aye aye, sir," in reply. The rest of the check went well but the last landing into Melbourne was unfortunately a 'thumper.' "Getting tired, Captain," Bruce said, but this time in a friendly manner with no emphasis on 'Captain.' All I had to do now was survive Day Two.

The next day was easier. Because Bruce was just 'observing', he ceased to ask any questions and I was lucky in having a very competent co-pilot and engineer. Both tried to help me in every way possible, even the weather was onside for a change. On landing back in Melbourne and after shut-down, Bruce leaned forward and said, "You better put these on your shoulder," and passed me the coveted four-bar epaulets. It took a while to sink in, I think mainly because I was mentally exhausted. There was no debrief – Bruce said that everything he had wanted to say had been said. "Go home and have a beer," was his parting advice and I did – several, in fact.

On reflection, my first paid commercial flight as a pilot was in December 1971, my first jet command as an airline pilot, October 1990, nearly 19 years later. Some apprenticeship! And one of the reasons pilots get upset when called glorified bus drivers.

11
LINE CAPTAIN
1990–1995

"Nice to meet one of my wombat Captains."
Sir Peter Ables, November 1990

One of my first trips as a brand-new Captain was a single sector Adelaide to Melbourne. Ron Hare was the flight engineer. Ron was one of the more senior engineers – he was well known for not suffering fools, was involved with the engineer's union and could be intimidating to junior crew. Adelaide, at the time, only had standoff parking bays with mobile stairs for boarding. Ron was waiting for me at the base of the stairs. I had just received the weather and flight plan and had ordered the fuel with Flight Operations. On this occasion there was a particularly strong high-altitude jet-stream with winds of up to 150 knots. With tailwinds of this magnitude, 18,000 lbs of fuel was all we needed. It costs fuel to carry any excess and the company frowned on unnecessary extra.

"Bars look a little shiny, Captain," Ron said as I approached the stairs, and then asked how much fuel I wanted. When I told him 18,000 lbs, he looked me straight in the eye and said, "Captain

Georgie, I don't go anywhere with less than 21,000 lbs in this 'ere aeroplane." "Well, today will be a first because that's all we need," I replied, and walked past him and up the stairs. It was customary to load the fuel evenly across both wing tanks and the fuselage centre tank. When it came to the pre-start checklist, the first officer reached the fuel check and Ron said, "Three sevens are 18." This annoyed me, and we flew to Melbourne with little conversation.

On arriving with well over all the legal reserves in place (even if we had left with 18,000 lbs) I pulled Ron to one side and said, "Don't ever do that to me again." I never had any further trouble with him, and we became good friends.

For junior captains, one common roster sequence was to fly the one and only 727 freighter. This was used primarily on a night freight run between Melbourne and Perth. Horse charters occurred at times and there were occasional trips to Tasmania. I enjoyed the freighter and have always liked night flying. The weather tends to be better, there is little other traffic about and it's generally a more relaxed atmosphere.

The freighter was registered VH-RMX and was fondly known by the crews as Ready Mix after the concrete company of the time. On the side of the nose of the aircraft was a painting of a wombat. All the 727 pilots agreed for a nominal amount to be deducted from their pay (from memory, around five dollars a month) and this money was used to support the wombats at the Melbourne Zoo. At the Zoo there was a plaque saying something along the lines of – 'These wombats are kindly funded by the pilots of Ansett Air Freight.'

What is not commonly known is the origin of the wombat connection. Since the early days of the Lockheed Electra, a four-engine turbo-prop freighter, the Air Freight pilots were jokingly referred to by all as wombats because 'they come out at night, eat roots and leave.' Along the way, the Electra gained the nose art of a wombat. Sir Peter Ables of TNT, who along with Rupert Murdoch of

News Ltd became the new owners of Ansett, approved the tradition to continue. It was said that Sir Peter thought it was 'very funny.' I met him in person once, outside a hotel in Sydney while waiting for the crew transport. When he learned I was on the 727, he patted me on the back and with a huge grin said, "Nice to meet one of my wombat Captains."

Post dispute, the bidding system in Ansett changed to a rotating one and this had the effect of being a fairer distribution of the flying. We also flew more, almost doubling our annual average of flying hours. The Boeing 727 was considered a dinosaur by this time, but I consider it a highlight of my flying career. Darwin overnights again proved to be highly sociable events with practical jokes the norm. A live mud crab placed in a co-pilot's bed was one of the more memorable. In retrospect, a little childish but the crews formed a bond not found on the other fleets.

I also flew with my first female co-pilot, Kamma Lynn, who proved to be a real character. Small in stature, she proved to be a very capable pilot and went on to gain a command on the Boeing 777 with a large Middle Eastern airline – no small achievement in my book. A rare smoker among the pilot ranks, Kamma would occupy spare moments in the cockpit by carefully rolling her own cigarettes using packet tobacco. Ansett had introduced a 'no smoking policy' some years previously.

I was once rostered for a licence renewal in the simulator with Kamma, and I found out years later that the pairing was deliberate. Apparently, the Blue Heeler wanted to make sure his slightly built captain and even smaller co-pilot could handle a Manual Reversion. The 727 had engine hydraulic pumps on only two of its three engines. If left with only the number three engine (right-hand side), the flight controls were no longer hydraulically powered. Control was now only via cables and the aircraft was extremely heavy to control in both pitch and roll. When faced with a total loss of hydraulics because of the loss of engines one and two,

Kamma and I were left with control forces which felt like concrete. Kamma wrapped both arms around the base of the control column and said, "Just tell me the pitch you want, and I'll give it to you." With Kamma controlling the pitch, I controlled the roll and we successfully landed the aircraft. "You two are quite an act," Bruce growled but it was great initiative from Kamma.

At Bruce's retirement function he admitted he wanted to make sure we could do it safely if ever paired together. He was a great Fleet Manager and highly respected by all the crews. We understood his demand for a high standard, and after a time realised that underneath the gruff exterior there was a man who genuinely cared for his pilots. We all pitched in and bought a fine trophy of a Blue Heeler Cattle Dog. I presented Bruce with this at his retirement function and he had a good chuckle over it. Apparently, he not only knew of his nickname, but he was also quietly proud of it.

I was promoted to a Training Captain and began to train new co-pilots on the aircraft. Now considered a dying fleet, we inherited some extremely low-time intake candidates with no previous jet time. The aircraft was less than ideal for this task in my opinion and I found it hard work. The aircraft was also becoming a victim of the 'noise abatement crowd.' The 727 was noisy compared to the new generation of aircraft entering the airlines but in its time was advertised as 'the whispering T-Jet!' Times were changing and the aircraft were quickly banned from Coolangatta.

The Mayor of Marrickville, an inner Sydney suburb, was another protagonist. When departing from Sydney to the north, we faced some restrictions including taking off at a reduced thrust setting. On safety grounds the captain always had the final say and I am ashamed to admit there were occasions of 'bad behaviour.' "Looks like the possibility of wind shear to me, Captain," the flight engineer would say. "Yes, I agree we better go full power," the Captain and Co-pilot would reply. The aircraft would then thunder across the roof of the Town Hall, rattling the mayor's windows and leaving behind three great long black soot trails, like a giant 'finger' – the finest 'up yours' ever invented.

In time, all the homes around Sydney airport were fitted with double glazing and roof insulation at a cost of millions to the government. So, in the end, the people who built or bought long after the airport was constructed had a win.

The 727 produced some real characters. Geoff Dempster was one captain who owned an art gallery, wore a brightly coloured sports coat complete with a cravat and rode a gold Harley-Davidson motorcycle. I remember him once turning up for a training course wearing green shoes! Dick McIntosh was another, who in his spare time owned and operated an ex-Indian Air Force Mig-21 jet fighter. One day, descending in the MiG, his cockpit canopy departed with a loud bang. Completely exposed to the howling slipstream and sitting like a peg on a clothesline, Dick calmly landed the aircraft and taxied in as if nothing had happened. Totally unflappable, Dick had the habit of calling everybody 'shags' and always wore his uniform hat at a rakish angle.

The F/Os were no different. One, Rick Hull, who looked about sixteen, was idolised by the young flight attendants and had a penchant for practical jokes. He once turned up for a flight with me, wearing very thick reading glasses. He explained the results from his last medical were such that he now needed glasses. I thought they looked a little thick, but I accepted his explanation. During the flight, shortly after the coffee arrived, I glanced over towards him and was astonished to see coffee spinning around the inside of his lenses! The glasses were from a joke shop. They had hollow frames and via a hidden drinking straw, Rick could get the coffee to flow through and create this bizarre effect. He had me in stitches. One flight engineer would wear a baseball hat with a rotating propeller on the top. Because he would be exposed to the First-Class passengers when the cockpit door was open, I had to ask him to remove it when the cabin crew were about to enter. They were wonderful flying companions, but some of them were totally mad.

One memorable event during my time on the 727 was an opportunity to fly the famous Fokker F-VIIb/3m, the aircraft used by Sir Charles Kingsford-Smith to pioneer the Pacific crossing. The aircraft was, in fact, a replica and operated by a few ex-Ansett pilots and sponsored by a South Australian Bank. Tony Mooy, from my Airlines of South Australia days, was one of two pilots managing the aircraft and they were looking for suitable candidates to complete an endorsement. They wanted pilots with previous radial engine tail-wheel time. The only small print was the applicant had to pay for the training at an estimated cost of $5,000. What an offer! The only problem was I could not afford that sort of money as we were in the process of building a new house, among other things. Help came from a surprising quarter. My mother-in-law offered to pay with no strings attached. I was humbled by her generosity and took perhaps too little time to say 'yes'!

11 June 1995 found me at the Adelaide domestic terminal in one of the Ansett offices with Colin Watt and Tony Mooy who conducted a very detailed briefing along ground school lines. All systems and limitations were covered and by the end of the day I was considered ready for the aeroplane. The next day we turned up at Parafield and began the preparation to fly the aircraft. Impressively large with its three radial engines pointing to the sky, it was not only a 'taildragger' but seemed to have a rudder far too small for its size. I thought quietly to myself – this thing is going to be a handful.

The aircraft proved to be not as bad as I first thought, except that the noise was almost unbearable; it seemed even nosier than the Bristol Freighter. There was only a windshield, the side windows were open and exposed. The only way to turn the aircraft in the air was to lead with the rudder and balance with the ailerons. Any slip or skid was rewarded with an icy blast of cold air mixed with engine oil rushing through the open cockpit. A better way to encourage balanced flight is hard to imagine.

Everything seemed to happen at 80 knots, including climb, cruise and descent. Landings were reasonably straightforward, with the combination of a lockable tailwheel and cantered mainwheels to help keep it running true. There was a hint of a 'swing' as the speed slowed with the tail down, but a touch of brake prevented anything sinister from happening.

After two days of flying from both seats, Tony was happy to sign me off and I was proud to have it on my licence. One thing the endorsement did was to make me think of the incredible feat of flying this contraption across the Pacific. I now hold an even greater respect for the early pioneers. The jury is out on whether they were extremely brave, extremely crazy or a healthy mix of both. I suspect the latter.

For the next few months, life fell into a very pleasant routine. I was asked if I would move base to Sydney and accept a 767 command. This I agreed to, only to have two captains lodge a complaint that it was out of seniority. Ansett no longer used direct line seniority but had adopted a complicated Experience Number based on the number of flight hours meeting various conditions. No point in explaining in any detail here but it was open to interpretation and caused many disputes. The outcome in my case was to be removed from the 767 course but retain a Sydney base on the 727. The Manager of Flight Operations, Alf Gloster was very apologetic and promised to "look after me at the next bid." This ended up being a lucky break, because once allocated a bid, the successful bidder was 'frozen' from bidding off type for five years. With all competition 'ring-fenced' and coming up for five years on the 727, I was in a prime position to fly the largest aircraft ever flown by Ansett. This was none other than the Boeing 747, the Queen of the Skies.

Ansett had been fighting to gain access to overseas routes for many years. The company had been flying on behalf of other airlines for some time, mainly small operations in the Pacific. These included Air Vanuatu, Airlines of the Cook Islands and Polynesian Airlines. Despite this, Ansett had been denied overseas routes in its own right for many years. This was deemed the sacred territory of Qantas and was untouchable. With the merger of Qantas and Australian Airlines (the former TAA) Ansett's domestic competitor, restrictions on Ansett were finally released.

Ansett's inaugural international flight in its own right occurred on 11 September 1993 – a relatively short hop to Denpasar, Indonesia. An ironic date if ever there was one. Eight years later in 2001, on the same day, Muslim terrorists attacked the World Trade Centre. The fallout spelled the end of Ansett International with the company ceasing operations five days later. But all this was in the future. In the meantime, Ansett consolidated its flights to Bali which proved highly successful. For the crews involved, it was a tough introduction, the destination attracting the 'lower end' of the market. 'Bogans to Bali' became the nickname for the pairing and coupled with a long tour of duty 'back of the clock', it quickly lost its allure.

Ansett subsequently announced further international expansion and that they were leasing three 747-300s from Singapore Airlines. Daily runs to Kansai in Japan and Hong Kong, in what is now China, were expected to start late 1994. The first aircraft arrived on 28 August 1994. The initial conversion of Ansett pilots through none other than our main competitor, Qantas, was not a happy experience. The failure rate in the simulator reached 47 per cent and included one 707 Fleet Manager. Ansett at the time had a Boeing 707 operating out of Hong Kong as a freighter under the company name of Transcorp.

On 19 October, Ansett had an unfortunate accident during a three-engine return to land in Sydney. With the number one engine shut down due to an oil leak, a combination of low power and being a little hot and high meant that the nose wheel did not have time to fully extend. The aircraft landed with the nose wheel retracted and all hell broke loose. During the subsequent investigation Ansett was accused of rushing the aircraft into service, not having adequate manuals and inadequate training of the crew. While the captain on the flight was an experienced ex-Cathay Pacific pilot, the first officer, Will Rogerson, was under training and the flight engineer, Les Bennett, was on his first trip following clearance to line. An unfortunate combination, exasperated by the loss of the engine, a rushed return and further bad luck followed.

When the aircraft broke cloud, two transmissions to warn the aircraft from separate sources jammed each other out. As they say, 'the holes lined up' that day. Poor old Will was the co-pilot on a very nasty engine failure on the 727. Having another major incident affected him greatly. He would quietly give up flying some years later. A true victim of the system in my book.

I was to later fly with Les Bennett, and he was an excellent engineer. He too suffered from the ignominy of being called, 'can't count Les.' During the confusion over the status of the landing gear, on answering the captain's query, Les replied, "Four greens" – he needed five. It is alleged the captain thought he said, "All greens." Sometimes you cannot make this stuff up. Qantas were quick to label Ansett, "F-Troop" after the popular TV comedy show depicting a useless American Army unit. It was not a good time to be an Ansett pilot under the watchful gaze of Qantas.

By the time the third aeroplane had arrived in November 1995, I was offered a position. This surprised many senior pilots but I was out of my freeze period on the 727 where much of the competition was still 'locked-in on type.' Other factors were the high failure rate and the fact it was an old analogue cockpit seemed to scare a few off from bidding. The so-called computer cockpits were making their presence even more, especially the new Airbus A320, which looked like the Star-Ship Enterprise in comparison. Many friends told me it would be bad for my career and in any case, there was a good chance of failure. Such faith was overwhelming!

On the analogue question, I liked the 'round dials' of old, was not mesmerised by the new technology and had discovered the world of the 'three crew cockpit'. I liked the flight engineer being in the operation, I had a strong background of old aeroplanes and there was no way I was not going to give it a try. Bids were made to now train with Qantas in Sydney, Air New Zealand in Auckland and United Airlines in Denver. Guess which straw I drew? Qantas in Sydney, of course.

12
FLYING THE BOEING 747
1995–2001

There is perhaps no other commercial airliner as iconic as the 747.
Martin Bowman, author of *Boeing 747, A History*

My last flight on the 727 was on 30 October 1995. A week later I was signing into the Qantas training centre in Sydney. Two first officers and another captain made up our course. The other captain, Terry Blair, was a Canadian I had not met before. He was the ex-Chief Pilot of the Canadian Company Conair, a large firefighting outfit. He had vast previous experience, including obtaining a DC-8 command at the young age of 28. Together with the unknown reception we would receive from Qantas and Terry's qualifications, I began to feel a little underconfident. I had nothing to fear and Terry and I quickly struck up a friendship that exists today. He was a total aviation enthusiast, and together with a very dry sense of humour we had much in common. Together, all four of us, like lambs to the slaughter, went upstairs to meet our Qantas mentors. It was nothing like I expected – they were very professional, helpful and seemed keen to get us through.

Once again, the usual endorsement routine dropped on our heads like a sledgehammer. Ground school and simulator sessions completely took over our lives on an almost 24-hour schedule. Again, it was like trying to drink out of a fire hose – so much to learn in such a short time. Terry proved to be an excellent companion as did the two F/Os and we all knuckled down and burned the midnight oil. Terry posted a cockpit layout on the wall of his room, known by all trainees as a Cardboard Bomber. We spent hours trying to bed down Qantas procedures. When procedurally operating the aircraft, radios had to be 'tuned', headings 'selected' and courses 'dialled' – nothing else was acceptable. I found this extra layer of SOPs difficult but quickly picked it up. Qantas left nothing open to interpretation. I found it a little anal at first but slowly came around to their way of doing it. The training overall was excellent and the simulator instructors were total gentlemen. All the horror stories did not eventuate.

During one lunch break it was suggested we visit the aircraft in the flesh as our latest arrival was parked at a remote stand opposite the corporate jet area. Free standing with a set of stairs to the forward entrance door, the aircraft looked enormous. Stopping halfway up the stairs and looking along the top of the wing we quickly decided it *was* enormous! On reaching the cockpit, the eye height out of the forward window was like being on the second floor of the terminal. I remember saying to Terry, "God, how are we ever going to land this thing from way up here?" "If Qantas can, we can," Terry replied. I loved his positive attitude; I needed that because I felt I had bitten off more than I could chew.

We all passed the exams without difficulty; the aircraft itself was beautifully designed with all the systems seemingly very logical. In recent years, two A380 Captains have both told me, "The 747 is over-engineered," – maybe they are right. I do not have sufficient engineering background to comment. The A380 only has two 5,000psi hydraulic systems, only two engines capable of reverse where the 747 has four 3,000psi hydraulic systems and all four engines have reverse thrust. There is no doubt the A380, in the software department, is a far superior product, but I always felt safe in the 747. You were surrounded by back-up systems; nothing seemed to box you into a corner. One engine out required a slight altitude loss and roughly 10 per cent more fuel for planning purposes but all in all, no big deal. Two engines out on one side required energy management on final approach, mainly not getting too slow but once the technique was understood, no problem. It was even possible to go-around with two engines out on the same side if you had the height to trade-off speed. The engineer's panel on the 747-300 was also a similar layout to the 727, procedures also much the same. Fuel management was more complex due to greater fuel loads and number of fuel tanks. Management from the captain's point of view of cross-checking the flight engineer was quite simple once you understood the configurations. Just prior to take-off, a quick glance of the cross-feed and tank selections forming an 'H' pattern was all that was needed.

After two and a half months of ground school and simulator training, we were finally ready to fly the real thing. We were rostered to ferry the aircraft from Sydney to Avalon, complete some circuit work and then ferry the aircraft back to Sydney. The cost of this exercise must have sent the accountants straight to the drinks cabinet.

With only five of us on board, I distinctly remember wandering about the cabin trying to decide where the best seat in the house was. On reaching Avalon we all completed a few circuits and the aeroplane proved to be easy to fly, providing you flew by the numbers. It still looked ridiculously high off the ground, but a radio altimeter call-out greatly assisted. The radio altimeter had a voice activated call-out and could be set to any altitude below 1500 feet.

Most operators opted for 1000, 100, 50, 30, 20 and 10 feet. On the 50-foot call-out, sink-rate was reduced and by the 30-foot call-out a gentle flare with power reduction produced some nice landings. A pussycat compared to the unforgiving 727. Thus began a love affair that would last 15 years. I really did feel a genuine affection for this gentle giant – what a wonderful testament to aeronautical engineering this aeroplane was.

Line-training commenced the following week, my first trip was to Hong Kong. My training captain, Lanny Jones, was an American, ex-Braniff Airlines and very laidback in that American way. Hong Kong at the time was still using Kai Tak, an overcrowded single runway airport with a unique and famous approach called an IGS (Instrument Guidance System). The approach to the commonly used runway 13 ended up requiring the sighting of a large red and white checkerboard mounted on the side of a hill. This was followed by a 47-degree right turn to align with the runway. With the aircraft turning close to the ground below the surrounding buildings, it was necessary to follow a sequence of flashing strobe lights in downtown Kowloon. Providing there was not a strong southerly wind trying to take you to the wrong side of the centreline, it was all quite doable. There was no margin for error and several operators proved this most convincingly. The results of getting it wrong varied from a simple pod strike where an engine pod struck the ground to several operators ending up in Kowloon Bay. One Chinese airline 747 (almost brand new) ended up in the bay and had its tail blown off by the Port authorities because it represented a shipping hazard, a fate I am sure the aircraft's makers never envisaged.

At the time of my training, Ansett served Hong Kong, Kansai in Japan and Kuala Lumpur in Malaysia. Within months, the network expanded to Seoul in Korea and Chiang Kai Shek airport in Taiwan.

After two months of line training, I was finally ready for my check to the line. This was completed by Keith Wallace with a Sydney – Hong Kong – Sydney sector. I had flown with Keith many times on both the F-27 and B-737. I knew he took no prisoners, but by the same token he was always fair. Unfortunately, both our American companions on the course failed to complete the training and returned to the A320 and B-737 respectively. Terry and I as the survivors became even closer. The differences between a pass and a fail could be exceedingly small at times and no way did I feel superior in any way; lucky to have a smooth check-ride would be a better description.

12.1 Ansett 747, Kansai. Photo taken by Tommy Mogren.

One of the Americans had a last-minute runway change on departure from Sydney. They re-programmed the PMS (Performance Management System as it was called on the 300) correctly but they failed to change the course bar for the initial runway track on the mode control panel. Confusion reigned on take-off with the classic 747 not being equipped with CRT screens that gave a more visual orientation. It was enough to set the tone on the wrong side of the ledger. A few small mistakes down-line, that in isolation would not be a failure just added to the score, resulting in the flight being marked down as below standard. I felt deeply sorry for him and tried to encourage him to have another go. Completely demoralised, he elected to return to his previous type. I felt this was a classic demonstration on the unforgiving nature of this flying business. Nothing is a given, experience and competence counted but did not include having a bad day.

I quickly discovered having a level of general fitness helped. I also discovered not having a big overnight before the flight home with a good night's sleep was essential. All well and good in theory, but the inevitable room party throwing the rules out the window sometimes! Long-haul flying incorrectly managed could be incredibly fatiguing. I started to have back problems sitting still for seven or eight hours with only a toilet break for exercise. Somehow, I adjusted, settled down and morphed into a long-haul pilot. The domestic pilots called us the Blue-Water Boys; we returned the favour by calling them the Yacht Club.

A new experience to add to my repertoire was typhoons. The typhoon season was referred to as JASON by the crews; that is, July, August, September, October and November. During this period, large tropical lows would develop into typhoons in the eastern Pacific and then turn westward before finally swinging up to the north and even back in an easterly direction. Generally speaking, in the air we simply went around them but once in the vicinity of the airport all hell broke loose. I remember being trapped in the Hyatt Hotel on Rokko Island in Japan on a Kansai layover. The co-pilot and cabin manager were helping me demolish the mini bar when we decided it was probably safe to venture outside. On reaching the foyer we were surprised to see a plastic chair fly past the front glass doors a good six feet off the ground. In the interests of safety, we retreated to the bar. Typhoons just required sitting out.

Even though my upbringing had a strong Asian background, I still found the North Asian cities daunting. The sheer number of people involved was mind-numbing. Nine million people in Seoul, seven million in Hong Kong and an unbelievable twenty-six million in Shanghai. I found the streets of Hong Kong claustrophobic. It was just a sea of human beings, wall to wall. It was impossible to walk at a standard pace; it was always dictated by the person in front of you. Many of the crew loved the place and I must admit I enjoyed it initially but eventually, the pollution got to me. I often had a sore throat and itchy eyes from the thick smog. It reminded me of the time the famous comedian Bob Hope landed in Hong Kong during the Vietnam War. On stepping out onto the tarmac, Bob said, "What is that goddam awful smell?" "It is shit, Sir," said his minder. "I know that," Bob replied, "but what have they done to it?" I thought Bob Hope summed it up nicely.

The Japanese were quite different; everything seemed very orderly, clean and under control. All the Customs Officers wore a powder-blue uniform complete with white gloves. The floors of the terminals were highly polished and traffic wardens with lighted batons seemed everywhere. They were exceptionally polite, but I often wondered what they really thought behind all those smiles. One thing I did enjoy was the Japanese food, and Ansett crews became regulars at the local sushi bars. At one establishment we befriended the owners to the point where their adult son came and stayed with my family in Brisbane. Later when we were living in Singapore, their whole family came to visit us. Very touching, and proof that if you can remove all the barriers of language and religion, people are the same the world over.

Life once again became a pleasant routine. I found the three-crew concept a great operation, as the flight engineer took care of the aircraft systems, and managed the fuel and engine logs. The first officer when not flying the sector, kept the flight plan running, programmed the INS (Inertial Navigation System) and kept a steady stream of coffee coming from the cabin crew. The job of the captain was to keep an eye on the big picture, especially changing weather and fuel burn. When all cockpit crew were working well together, it was an extremely efficient team.

After two years of this agreeable lifestyle, things started to take a turn. The company had three 747-300s and began to look at converting to the more fuel-efficient 400 model. Even more disturbing, route rationalisation was being mooted with the fleet reduced to two 747-400s. Ansett international also had two 767s. Since I had been recruited for the third 747, it looked like I would lose my slot and go onto the 767.

A lifeline was offered in the form of a temporary transfer to Singapore Airlines for 12 months. They too were in the process of getting rid of the older 747-300 models and needed additional crew while their own crews converted to the 400. The contract deal resulted in a slight pay drop, but I grabbed it to stay on type. Type conversion courses were stressful exercises and I had no interest in the 767. Singapore wanted eight crews but only two Ansett crews volunteered due to the loss in pay. The airline eventually found the extra six crews from South African Airways. The two Ansett captains were Graham Henry and myself, and the two first officers were Scotty Fleming and David Thorn. My wife fully supported the move, and so we prepared to move and live in Singapore. We decided not to rent out our home but to leave it empty for 12 months while paying for pool and garden maintenance.

13
A YEAR IN SINGAPORE
1998–1999

"You are mad to go there for less money."
Fellow Ansett 747 Captain, January 1998

In early March 1998, the four of us found ourselves in the Roxy Hotel on the east coast of Singapore Island. All attempts to avoid another conversion course were met with the news that the Singaporean CAAS (Civil Aviation Authority of Singapore) required us to do the complete course again. We also had to pass an aviation law exam. The Chief Pilot of the 747-300 fleet was Captain S. Y. Chow, commonly known as SY. He was a most charming individual, softly spoken and extremely helpful in integrating us newcomers into their system. It was, however, back to head down and bum up.

Once again Computer Based Training (CBT) ground school and hours of simulator work. The Singaporeans were very thorough, more so than even Qantas. While some of it was over the top, I was extremely impressed with their standard, especially their systems knowledge. In some ways they were very reminiscent of the old way of doing things with quite a few sessions of chalk and talk. The aviation law exam was a different matter and difficult, with one of our English companions failing it. A bit of rough justice for the Australians, as the exam was based on the English aviation law. This little gem still contained rules for airships and rigid dirigibles, including airship mooring regulations. One question required a bearing from another aircraft worked out from the position of its navigation lights. "Typical Pommy bullshit," said Scotty in his eloquent style. I must say I agreed with him.

13.1 Secondment to SIA – Graeme Henry, S. Y. Chow, George Palmer, David Thorn, Scotty Flemming.

The whole process took over two months and included acquiring US certification as several of their aircraft were on the US register. When it came to the full-flight simulator, the Ansett pilots were not paired together but rostered with one of our newfound friends from South African Airways. S. Y. Chow felt this would help dilute our previous airline procedures and make it easier to adjust to the Singaporean way of doing things. I was paired up with a South African pilot who proved to be a great partner, but I did have trouble with his strong Afrikaans accent. "The pork brake is sit," he would say. Despite these language problems, we all passed the course successfully.

Finally, on 10 June 1998, I flew one of their aircraft for the first time when I conducted some circuit training at Changi. Captain Eddy Kway completed my conversion process in 747-300 registration N122KH. Eddy Kway had a reputation of being a hard-arse on check-rides but I found him to be more than fair. He was a large man and intimidating in appearance but had a keen sense of humour. He ended up doing my line training and we got on well. I think his knowledge that I had grown up in Singapore helped, and we discussed the rapid development of Singapore at length. It was here I learned that my old school was now a brewery. I am sure my old headmaster would have been most impressed.

My final check-out consisted of a return flight from Singapore to Manila. This route took the aircraft close to the ITCZ (The Inter Tropical Convergence Zone). This is where the northeast and southeast trade winds converge near the equator. Coupled with the monsoon, this area could produce thunderstorms of Biblical proportions. The flight number (SQ72/73) was known amongst the crews as 'the thriller to Manila.' I received much sympathy from my compatriots when they discovered the route I had for the all-important check. The test itself proved straightforward and most of the thunderstorms conveniently sat either side of our track. I flew to Manila like Moses parting the Red Sea. My check-captain was a Captain Cotting, an ex-chief pilot of Swiss Air. Captain Cotting was a glider enthusiast and an all-round professional aviator. It was a pleasure to fly with him and he kindly released me into the system.

Once assigned a normal roster, I began to fly to places I had only dreamed of. India and the Middle East featured predominately and exotic places like Istanbul in Türkiye. There I visited the Blue Mosque and stood in total awe at the incredible ceiling under the main dome. I spent time in the famous bazaars and even hired a car with a driver to visit the Gallipoli Peninsula. After being driven for four hours from Istanbul, I found this to be one of the more moving experiences of my life. It is one of the few World War I battlegrounds left untouched since the cessation of hostilities. The scale of the casualties and the visible remains of the trenches brought tears to my eyes. Placing my hand into the sand on Anzac Cove I quickly found expended ammunition and bone fragments. I left my discoveries where I found them and left the site trying to understand the reasons why. What a waste of young lives, and for what gain? This was the very beach my grandfather had shelled from the Battleship Queen Elizabeth. If only human beings could learn to live with each other.

One other regular destination was Dacca, the capital of Bangladesh. We would leave late evening for the four-hour flight arriving around midnight. The approach to runway 14 was complicated as the procedure included tracking outbound from one navigation aid to join the Instrument Landing System (ILS). There were no radar services provided by this impoverished country. Airport security seemed lax and it was not unusual to see people running into the grass in the glare of the landing lights. You had to be careful on the narrow taxiways to avoid dropping a wheel into the grass, especially during a turn.

Refuelling was from a truck guarded by an armed soldier. On approaching the refueler to complete the paperwork, the guard would offer a smart salute. I would go out of my way to be pleasant to these people as they seemed terrified of authority. The passengers were invariably young men in blue overalls and we would pick up as many as 300 at a time. They were on their way for contract labouring jobs in Singapore. These poor devils would be housed in converted shipping containers and no doubt poorly paid. An important part of driving the Singapore economy but to me no more than slave labour. The whole experience made me appreciate how lucky I was to have had the opportunities in life presented to me. I would always treat these people with the same respect as any first-class passenger.

Melissa and I lived in the Shangri-La Hotel on Sentosa Island. The short contract of one year meant that this was a practical option. The other pilots did the same, including the South Africans who joined us later. We lived in a style more reminiscent of the old colonial days, including gin and tonics on the veranda! Looking back at the period, both my wife and I think 1998 was the best year of our lives. We had an absolute ball, met people from all over the world and lived like kings. The Ansett pilots who declined the transfer on grounds of a slight pay drop proved to me that not everything is about money.

14
BACK TO ANSETT
1999–2001

"Where have you been?"
Terry Blair, Ansett Check Captain, February 1999

February 1999 found us back in Australia, and revalidated into the Ansett system. Due to natural attrition over the last 12 months, I found to my surprise that I rated a slot on the newer 747-400 model. Some senior pilots were coming out of their freeze periods, and some doubt about my survival on the aircraft type remained. What saved me was the company considering the 400 a replacement type and not a new bid. Other factors were an age limit of 60 in order to recoup training costs before the compulsory retirement age of 65 for international operations. Hanging on to my position by a thread, I once again was rostered to train with Qantas.

By now I was becoming almost a permanent student on conversion courses and settled in quickly. The queue to replace me if I stumbled was long. Gone was the flight engineer, his panel was now relocated in the pilot's overhead position. The Inertial Navigation System was replaced with three Inertial Reference Systems doing a similar job but with more accuracy and sophistication. In-built accelerometers used laser beams to measure movement. Two GPS units acted as a back-up and the round dials of the instrument panel were replaced with CRT screens. The course was long and hard, and again two pilots on our course of four failed to qualify.

I understood my own frailty by now. I no longer considered myself thick but needed to understand something to grasp it properly. I also needed more time to comprehend technical matters. I think the experts would call me a slow learner. I needed to go over material a second time. Armed with this new self-diagnosis, I resisted invitations to socialise and just lived for the course and passing it. It is a shame nobody worked this weakness out during my school years and offered assistance. I am now convinced rates of learning do indeed vary between individuals, and many good people fail only because they are left behind. A basic intelligence level is only half the battle.

My training captain for the 400 conversion was none other than my old course partner on the 300, Terry Blair. We had a very pleasant time together and I was cleared to the line shortly after. In August of the same year, I was asked if I would like to be a Training Captain myself on type. I agreed and trained in the simulator to operate from both the left and right seats to enable the training of other captains.

In 2000, the Olympic Games came to Sydney and Ansett became the official carrier for the games. The Olympic torch was flown from Greece to Sydney with much pomp and fanfare in one of Ansett International's 767s. One 747-300 was painted up in Olympic colours and later a 400 was painted in a toned-down scheme. Half of the rear fuselage of the 300 was painted in a very stylised royal blue blending into the white of the forward fuselage. Giant 'Sydney 2000' lettering in white was overwritten on the blue section together with the Olympic logo. This was all "very exciting" to the public relations staff and the advertising agency. There was only one small problem.

The '2' looked more like a 'Z' in its trendy script and the last '0' was painted over the rear left exit door (door 5L). Door five was a common entry point for servicing the aircraft, both catering and cleaning. With the door open 'Sydney 2000' quickly became 'Sydney Zoo.' We copped quite a bit of ridicule from another operator's crew but I think they were just jealous! I found it re-enforced my opinion that advertising people should be kept far away from aeroplanes. Some of today's colour schemes on aircraft are truly hideous and an eyesore. I once saw a 747 in Tokyo covered from nose to tail in large Pokémon cartoon characters. It looked totally ridiculous.

Ansett International continued to be a success and was now making a profit. The parent however, continued to struggle with a mixed fleet and high overheads. The company would survive for only a further two years. On 11 September 2001, Islamic terrorists attacked the US Trade Centre. At the time I was flying back from Japan and the Americans closed the airspace around Guam just as I was passing through. Not knowing the reason until I arrived home, I was shocked like everyone else to see the news. Flight cancellations followed and this proved to be the straw that broke the camel's back. By 14 September, a mere three days after the event, Ansett International shut down. I never flew an Ansett aeroplane again. The speed of the collapse made it even harder to comprehend. One minute I was a senior 747 captain with a successful airline and the next, unemployed.

The terrorist attack also caused a general downturn throughout the world and employment prospects looked bleak. While the industry did recover, it was never the same. Crews are now locked behind re-enforced cockpit doors protected by cameras. Airport security is now at a level where flying is a miserable and degrading experience for passengers and crew alike. Sadly, much of the security is theatre to satisfy political objectives. To industry professionals, there are still many giant gaps.

Oddly, the easiest places to transit are those directly affected, like New York. Some of the most unpleasant are places like Manchester in England. Despite denials to the contrary, security in Manchester appears much focused on aircrew. Every visit there was a humiliating experience. We were treated as potential terrorists, often by migrants from the sub-continent with no trace of an English accent. For somebody born in England, it was hard to take. An American pilot once said to me, "The definition of happiness is V1 at Manchester." V1 is the decision 'go or stop' speed during take-off; once V1 is reached, stopping within the remaining runway length is not guaranteed.

After I had spent two months writing to employment agencies, Captain S. Y. Chow of Singapore Airlines made contact and I was offered a job back with them. One of the easier decisions I have ever made. We packed our bags.

15
BACK TO SINGAPORE
2001–2011

"We don't necessarily want you here, we need you here."
Human Resources Manager, Singapore Airlines, January 2002

I arrived back in Singapore and you guessed it, I had to do the 400 Conversion Course all over again. By now I was past caring about officialdom. I was now a more mature 51-year-old with the spirit truly beaten out of me by the idiotic bureaucrats. If they wanted me to wear a pink dress, I would go down the road and buy one.

We were quickly joined by some ex-British Airways pilots. These colourful characters quickly became good friends. At the time, the retirement age for British Airways was 55, whereas Singapore was 60 (later increased to 62 for ex-pats, 65 for locals). This enabled recently retired BA crews an opportunity to keep flying for a few more years. The Singaporeans, on the other hand, were only too grateful for the experience. Despite this, we were shocked to be told at our induction, "We don't want you here, we need you here." At least they were honest. An early indication of cultural differences was the requirement to all stand together in the company theatre and sing the company song. The Singaporean Human Resources Manager was most impressed with the hearty response, not for a minute suspecting, that in fact, we were all taking the mickey. The memory of ex-BA Captain Glen Lomas, a giant Yorkshireman booming out, "Singapore Airlines, you are a great way to fly," will live with me forever!

Once again, the Ansett pilots were paired off with pilots from another airline in the simulator to help remove 'our way of doing things'. This time we were matched with the pilots from British Airways. I was rostered with a very pukka BA pilot and it is amusing to record the adjustment required from both sides.

One of the principal methods of flying the 747 with the autopilot engaged is via a Mode Control Panel (MCP) which was located the width of the upper instrument panel. The panel has various selector buttons suitably labelled. One is a pitch mode referred to as Flight Level Change. At Ansett, strange as it may sound, we called it Flight Level Change. In British Airways, they called it as labelled on the button, FLCH, pronounced FLITCH. On descent, while manually hand-flying, my erstwhile companion got a little 'hot and high' and, in one of those not uncommon situations in the simulator, needed another mode and quickly. "Could I have FLITCH, please?" he said, in his very upmarket accent. I replied in my Australian drawl; "No worries, I'll give you FLITCH if you tell me what the bloody hell it is." We both ended up laughing and still managed to resurrect our slightly out of control aeroplane.

The instructor was not amused. He was a different kettle of fish to our beloved S. Y. Chow. He barely disguised his dislike of ex-pats, was very surly and liked everything in a strict order. He showed a lack of lateral thinking and could be very anal to the point of stupidity at times. He was horrified by our relaxed style and method of doing things. Our antics, when we misunderstood each other, did not go down very well at all. We passed the simulator despite all of this and moved on to line training. We quickly learned that the best way to deal with the locals was to simply agree with them. After all, it was their airline. We used an expression, OIC, an abbreviation for "Oh I see!" Overall, I found their training excellent and did not have any problems doing it their way.

15.1 Boeing 747-400 Cockpit, Singapore Airlines.

Due to my previous time on type, line training consisted of one European pairing and one Pacific crossing to the US. All of this with a delightful ex-Hawker Hunter pilot from the Singaporean Air Force, John Norfor. He very generously signed me off with a good report. I was now released to the world of ultra-long haul flying. The 747-400 had an extra ten tons of fuel in the tailplane compared with the 300 model and was capable of Changi to London non-stop, a flight time of 14 hours. I began to fly both Atlantic and Pacific crossings and visited most of the major European cities.

I found the Middle East fascinating, but the heat could be unbearable with temperatures in the high forties. In Sharjah in the UAE, I even found the old fort used as a terminal back in Imperial

Airways days during the 1930s. It is now buried in the centre of town, the runway part of the main road. Here lumbering HP42s, giant biplanes powered by four radial engines, would land for fuel and overnight on their long journey to India.

One of the BA captains on our course was Simon Rendell, the son of a former Imperial Airways pilot who flew the HP42s. His father also flew with the famous Imperial Airways pilot O. P. Jones. I met his father at his home in London just before he died and his tales of flying in the 1930s were fascinating. He also flew Mosquitoes on the famous British Airways 'ball-bearing run', outrunning the Germans on a night run to Sweden. The reason for the flight was to ferry back vital ball-bearings needed in industry. Simon's brother Geoff was also an ex-BA pilot who flew the Concorde. After a brief introduction in London, we met up at White Waltham and had an enjoyable hour of circuits in his Tiger Moth biplane. White Waltham was a historic airfield from the war years used by the Air Transport Auxiliary. The ATA was a civilian organisation used extensively to ferry military aeroplanes from the factories to operational RAF Bases. A vast number of their pilots were female. Simon's daughter also flew VC-10 tankers in the RAF – they were a truly remarkable flying family. Simon and his wife Nancy became good friends with us and we had many enjoyable evenings together.

This second visit to Singapore was quite different to the one year in 1998. I was now flying both the passenger and the pure freighter version of the 747-400 series. The freighters literally went everywhere with freight hubs in Brussels for the European operation and Anchorage in Alaska for the North American network. A steady pattern developed where a week away and a week home became the norm.

My long-suffering wife was magnificent, and we decided to live in a hotel again to try and save some money. We ended up with a junior suite in the Beaufort Hotel on Sentosa Island which was later renamed the Sentosa Resort and Spa. Overlooking the sea on a cliff-top with a view of the Indonesian islands with the extensive lines of moored shipping, it was a truly idyllic spot. At night when sitting at the bar, one could watch the maritime version of my job. Unlike the glamorous aviation industry, our compatriots of the sea seemed to come and go without any fanfare. No wailing relatives at crowded and packed terminals with long queues. One evening they were parked out the front of the hotel and the next morning they were gone. Late at night I would watch their lights sliding slowly across the horizon; majestic and graceful they would just simply disappear into the dark.

One day I met an Australian first officer from a visiting oil tanker. His ship was dry-docked with a propeller change in the Jurong Shipyard. "Would I like a guided tour?" My quick reply soon had us both standing under the hull in the dry-dock. I was totally amazed at the scale of everything and the complete disregard for saving weight. Weight is the number one enemy of aviation, not so in the shipping industry. If a simple handrail weighed half a ton that is what it weighed, end of story. A visit to the bridge revealed some interesting comparisons. The captain proudly stated that his ship used 140 tons of fuel a day. I told him a flight from Singapore to London was 14 hours and we used 140 tons of fuel! He was just as fascinated as I was by the comparison. Their next trip was to carry a load of fuel oil to Townsville in Queensland, a trip of seven days. I told him that would take us seven hours! We had a very enjoyable day together, followed by a happy drinking bout that took me days to recover from. They were a hardy lot, those men of the sea.

16
FLYING THE LINE
2001–2011

"God damn, where are you from?"
Motorist offering me a lift, Anchorage Alaska,
-26 degrees Celcius, January 2003

The world quickly became my oyster, as they say, and the variety of destinations seemed endless. Looking through the pages of my logbook it is hard to imagine that I did go to all the places listed. One day lunch in Times Square, New York, the next, pork knuckles in Frankfurt. Two days later it could be curry in Calcutta (Kolkata) or noodles in Nanchang. It was an amazing experience, and one I never tired of.

Anchorage in Alaska was one destination that took me by surprise. On my first trip there, it was bitterly cold with a temperature of -26 degrees Celsius. I was told by my young co-pilot that in these temperatures boiling water would not reach the ground. Being a sceptic at heart I had to try and sure enough, after I poured boiling water from our parked aircraft door, not a drop reached the ground. It crackled and hissed like a child's sparkler. To finish this tale, I had to pay the co-pilot $20 for doubting him. One should not accept a bet based on ignorance! It was so cold I had difficulty breathing and it felt like my nose was full of toothpicks – a strange sensation caused by nasal hair freezing.

On one layover I tried to walk from the Hilton Hotel to Lake Hood, a home for countless seaplanes. I was soon in trouble despite wearing a double layer of clothing. A large SUV pulled over and the driver told me to jump in. "God, damn, where are you from?" the rugged-looking individual exclaimed. On telling him I was Australian, he said, "That figures," and went on to tell me you should never venture out without a hat or head covering. He had stopped as soon as he saw my blonde hair blowing in the breeze, identifying me as somebody in need of rescue! He very kindly not only took me to the Lake Hood aerodrome to visit the museum, but he also drove me back to the hotel. I bought him lunch in return.

The Alaskans were some of the most 'air-minded' people in the world. Even the female bartender at the Hilton owned an aeroplane! With only a few hours of daylight in the winter months, as well as snowstorms and earth tremors, it was not a place for the faint-hearted. On most flights we had to be de-iced, and had to be careful with all aspects of the operation. Taxi speeds above five knots would be asking for trouble on the icy taxiways and the turbulence on landing could be quite violent. I loved the place; they had a can-do attitude to everything. Whatever was needed to get the job done was just done that way, with no fuss. A few precious airport managers with their volumes of rules would do well to visit Anchorage.

Another aspect of the job was flying the world's great oceans. The North Atlantic was one that required separate route training with a training captain to qualify. Due to the high-density traffic and the strong winds so common with this part of the world, a highly organised system to control the air traffic was in place. This was called NATS or the North Atlantic Track System. Westbound, everybody wanted to get out of the strong headwinds and eastbound, everybody wanted to get in them to take advantage of the fuel savings. Six westbound and six eastbound tracks are published every six hours. Westbound are given a track designator alphabetically from A to F and Eastbound from the other end of the alphabetic starting with Z. The tracks are 60 miles apart (since my retirement, this has been further reduced to 30 miles under a 'reduced lateral separation minima') and the aircraft fly the same track in trail with 20 miles separation. Speed is regulated under a Mach technique procedure, which to a layman is simply a form of speed control. When looking on Flight Tracker websites, the aircraft appear like a giant daisy-chain slowly making its way across the Atlantic. The 747 was relatively fast with a cruising speed of Mach .86 (Mach 1.0 being the speed of sound). It was quite an art to reach the entry point of the NAT track at the correct allocated time and at the optimum level. Not to have a slower aeroplane in front was also a big advantage. The Boeing 767, for example, was slow at Mach .80 and so too was the Airbus A330 at .82.

Leaving Frankfurt westbound we immediately would work out who and what was ahead of us and try and jostle into the most advantageous position. We called A330s 'half-past threes' or 'roadblocks', and they were our principal opponent. I found it was best to stay low and fast to get underneath them and gain the coveted twenty miles separation. Once this was achieved, climb up, hopefully to the optimum level. One had to be careful not to infringe reserve fuel with the increase in fuel burn by staying down and going fast. If you could have an uninterrupted cruise speed at optimum altitude on the allocated track, it made a huge difference to the fuel burn and schedule.

This whole exercise required deft planning and judgment but was very satisfying if you managed to pull it off. This was a classical pilot exercise, where to a non-flyer it would seem as if the pilots were just sitting there watching the autopilot but were, in fact, remarkably busy. The tracks varied considerably according to the wind and I have been as far south as the Mid-Atlantic to get across. The passenger aircraft went to JFK on Long Island while the cargo flights went into Newark (EWK) on the mainland. The average time westbound from Frankfurt was around eight hours and eastbound seven hours due to the tailwinds.

A typical westbound trip would have us fly around 64 degrees north, just off the Greenland coast, crossing the Canadian coast around Goose Bay in Newfoundland. We would then track down the St Lawrence passage past Quebec and into mainland America. Overflying either Albany or Boston depending on the route, we would then fly the length of Long Island on descent into JFK. Long Island's name quickly becomes obvious as it is indeed an exceedingly long island! Full of history, especially aviation history, it contains many aerodromes and aviation manufacturing industries. New York itself was a veritable wasp's nest with high density traffic streaming into three major airports, Newark on the mainland, LaGuardia and JFK on the Island. Additionally, there were numerous other airports in the vicinity including Stewart to the north and Long Island on the island itself.

The New York controllers were famous for being fast talking, shoot from the hip types who took no prisoners. My ex-British Airways friends, in that classical English understated manner, called them, "quite rude." I had no problem with them, but you had to listen carefully to their rapid instructions.

Once I stopped the aircraft on a taxiway to check for myself the chart and the given directions to the terminal. "You got a problem, Singapore?" boomed the controller in his loud 'Archie Bunker' accent. On telling him I was double-checking the route, he replied, "That's fine, sir, you can stop and think anytime but just follow that Airbus in front and call the Ramp on 130.77."

Some of the conversations where English was not the pilot's first language were hilarious. I liked them; it was just the New York way of doing things. They were just the same everywhere, abrasive at times but underneath this rough facade they had a heart of gold. A concierge at a hotel once said, "You gonna keep looking at those fancy brochures or are you gonna ask me a question?" Not the same approach from the white-gloved, top-hatted concierge in London with his, "Good evening, sir. May I be of assistance?" It took me a while, but I am now a great fan of New York and its tough people.

On New York overnights, we stayed at the Sheraton Hotel on Times Square. During one layover, the co-pilot and I paid a visit to the World Trade Centre, or what was left of it. During my visit there they were still clearing the rubble. The scale of the disaster was readily apparent when you saw the area firsthand. Giant twisted steel beams looked like clawed fingers surrounded by mountains of rubble. The terrible smell was a surprise. We both left without a word being spoken. It was not an experience I relish, and, in some ways, I regret going there. I found it psychologically disturbing and it took a while to get it out of my head. Three thousand and three hundred people died on that site, more than at Pearl Harbour. It is easy to understand America's desire to hunt down the perpetrators. It is harder to comprehend the intensity of hatred these lunatics must have had to commit such an act. They like to be called Soldiers of Islam but there is nothing soldierly about killing innocent unarmed civilians, especially women and children. They were quick to hide in caves when real soldiers took them to task.

One of my more interesting Atlantic crossings was on 16 April 2010. During our overnight stay in Frankfurt, the Company Manager rang the hotel and asked if I could prepare the crew to leave earlier than scheduled. A volcano in Iceland with the unlikely name of Mount Eyjafjallokull had erupted with a massive ash cloud moving towards Europe. The French were considering closing all their airspace and the Germans would probably follow suit. It all seemed surreal until I turned on the news. Although the broadcast was in German, it did not take much to realise that this was no ordinary eruption. Looking like the effects of a nuclear explosion, ash clouds were already reaching 30,000 feet. Ash clouds consist of material similar to glass and have the ability to choke and fail a jet engine. Such a case occurred in Indonesia with British Airways. On 24 June 1982, a 747 of British Airways lost all four engines after flying into volcanic ash. Luckily, they managed to get engines re-lit and made a successful emergency landing into Jakarta. The cockpit windows were badly crazed reducing visibility to near zero – a remarkable save by the crew.

We managed to gather the crew and most of the booked passengers and prepared to depart. On the bus to the airport, we were informed that French airspace had indeed closed. I had to arrange a new flight plan that took us directly south through Germany and into Spanish airspace to bypass the closed French zone. My main concern was a plan B in case of an inflight emergency. The German Air Traffic Controllers gave an airborne time of less than an hour away and advised that we would be the last departure before German airspace was to close. I felt very vulnerable and that I was being rushed. Looking for support, I asked the co-pilot if he was happy and I received the classic reply, "It's up to you, Captain." I quickly saw there were good options to divert into Spanish airports, the weather was good and the route would take us over the Azores. This mid-Atlantic Island chain had several airports we could use as well. Satisfied that common sense prevailed, we somehow became airborne with two minutes to spare. Even so it was concerning to be advised by the controllers, "All German airspace is now closed, have a nice flight." The flight was uneventful and took 8 hours and 20 minutes, only an extra 20 minutes from normal but it was disorientating approaching New York on a north westerly heading. Needless to say, there was no sign of any ash cloud and all the flight attendants eventually paid a visit to the cockpit 'to have a look.' Unfortunately, the whole North Atlantic subsequently shut down and we were trapped in New York for six days. A week in New York as a paid tourist was a pleasant consolation prize.

16.1 Ansett Australia Boeing 747 300. Photo taken by Rob Finlayson.

16.2 SFO C. Tang, George Palmer, FO M. Huei, London, 29 Sept 2003.

Our European passenger destinations included London, Paris, Frankfurt, Munich, Copenhagen, Brussels, Madrid, Manchester and Zurich. As previously stated, I disliked Manchester although they did have an excellent aviation museum. One strange thing about Manchester was the instrument landing system had the same frequency of 109.5 for both ends of Runway 06L/24R. When they changed runways, they just switched the ILS (Instrument Landing System) to the opposite end. This was unusual, but effective. It was also a very noise-sensitive airport with no fewer than five noise monitoring stations just short of runway 06. The weather was always appalling, maybe just bad luck on my part, but I do not remember ever seeing the sun or blue sky at Manchester.

On 5 December 2006, I was called out at the last minute to crew SQ334/333 to Paris. This turned out to be the last rostered flight of a Singapore Airlines 747 to this beautiful city. The 747 was being replaced with the new A380. The flight was originally scheduled to be flown by the fleet manager and for some reason or other he could not make it. On our arrival in Paris at the hotel, we found the room was still booked in his name. With much arm waving, shock and dismay, the discrepancy was solved and I soon found myself in an upgraded suite. On the coffee table was a letter greeting the boss on this special occasion, complete with fruit, chocolates and two bottles of fine champagne. A bit of rough justice, I thought. Not wanting to offend the good offer from management, the rest of the crew helped to make short work of it.

Dublin was a freight destination; often the load was expensive racehorses being ferried from the Middle East to graze on the green fields of Ireland. This was to avoid the stifling desert heat during the hotter months. The runways were relatively short with only one of the three available suitable for a 747 and even then, it was only 8600 feet long. As a result, it always seemed to be a crosswind landing. Trying not to upset priceless horses on a short runway in a strong crosswind was a challenge. We tried not to use too much braking and reverse thrust, but it was not always possible. I always watched the horses going down the scissor-link when they were unloaded. I am sure some of those looks they gave me as they peered over the horse box with those big wide brown eyes said, "Have you really got a licence?"

Dublin was rare in that there was no dedicated crew channel for immigration. On reaching the front counter in full uniform, with my co-pilot in tow, the officer asked in his broad Irish accent; "And what is the purpose of your visit, sir?" I gave him what our American cousins would call 'a shit-eating grin'; he just smiled and said, "You boys have a lovely stay now," and waved us through. We stayed at the Marriott which had the biggest bar I have ever seen; you could drive a car around it. Here the locals would sit quietly drinking warm Guinness watching the sports channel on an elevated screen. It was a funny place.

Freighter rosters were not popular with the locals due to roster disruptions, as well as some patterns taking you away from home base for two weeks. One sequence literally flew around the world. I remember taxying in on return to Changi from such a trip and saying to the co-pilot, "Well there you go, Charles, the world is indeed round, we have been heading east for two weeks and we are back where we started from!" The odd look I received proved once again that western humour is not always understood. I am sure he told his pals that he flew with an Australian captain who thought the world was flat.

Zurich was another airport with an interesting procedure. Due to the early hour of our scheduled arrival, we could only use the short runway 28, complete with a non-precision approach. This was due to strict noise abatement regulations. Two great long runways equipped with ILS (Instrument Landing System) were not available unless the airport had low visibility procedures in place. The short runway resulted in the approach and landing being 'captains only' – it was deemed too difficult for an inexperienced co-pilot.

Having flown all night with minimum rest, it seemed crazy to me that we were forced into a less than ideal approach while critically tired.

What is more, due to the short length, we were obliged to use full-flap and full-reverse, so even the noise issue seemed pointless. One operator, flying a four engine BAE146 misread the manual step-down altitude and flew into the trees short of the runway, killing all on board. I am sure that made a noise as well. The rules were so strict we were not allowed to use the Auxiliary Power Unit (a small jet engine in the tail) to power us up on the ground. Compromising safety to appease people who insist on living at the end of runways has always been a sore point with me.

Zurich itself was a pleasant enough place and stunningly beautiful. I often took the ferry on Lake Zurich to Rapperswil, an old historic town on the northern edge of the lake complete with cobbled streets. On one hand, the Swiss jealously guarded their historical heritage and on the other, they had some of the weirdest modern architecture. Another area where the Swiss excelled was in bathroom design. They seemed hell-bent on having the strangest plumbing designs. Some of the bathroom taps were worthy of an aptitude test. Funny, single unit taps with multiple functions, not obvious until you scalded yourself with hot water. Foot pedals used to flush toilets, absolutely bizarre light switches and so on. When you arrived exhausted in an unfamiliar hotel room, you just did not need the 'Swiss tap and lights test.' When I lived in Air Force married quarters as a kid, the hot tap had a red H and the cold one had a blue C – what's wrong with that, Switzerland?

Out of the other European destinations, many pilots would admit to Paris being a favourite. I preferred Frankfurt in many ways. With the terrible losses my family suffered during the Second World War, this might seem a strange choice. The city itself was nothing in terms of architecture or choice of things to do, compared to Paris. It was the people. Big cities can be notoriously unfriendly, intimidating and lonely places, especially if you are wandering the streets alone at night. Walk into any bar or restaurant in Frankfurt, you were always made to feel welcome and were engaged by the locals. At the Frankfurt street markets, total strangers would offer you a seat at their table and buy you a drink. The Germans had a great sense of fun and seemed a happy lot. They, too, had a terrible history; Frankfurt was levelled during the war. Unexploded bombs are still found on building sites. Bomb splinter scars are still visible on the outside walls of the Central Railway Station. I quickly made friends with some of the restaurant staff and they treated me like family when I arrived on an overnight. I was even jokingly referred to as 'the escaped airman.'

The only downside was the weather: winter storms could produce some very heavy snowfalls. I took Liss with me on several trips and once left her in the hotel in Frankfurt to be picked up by me on my return from New York. The poor girl was trapped in the room for two days by deep snow, preventing any movement outside. At the airport, snowploughs would keep the runways open and the aircraft would be de-iced prior to departure. I have spent Christmas Day in Frankfurt and have fond memories of it. The atmosphere with their Christmas markets was unforgettable. Individual portable wooden buildings produced hot wine, pork knuckles and apple strudel for dessert. With snow falling outside, an open fireplace and a girl wearing traditional dress playing the accordion; it just does not get any better.

Munich was another German destination but only on the freighter. One memorable experience was catching a bus to Berchtesgaden and then onwards to visit Hitler's Eagle Nest. I have always found World War II history interesting, especially reflecting on the final outcomes. Built on the top of a mountain, Eagle's Nest was reached via an elevator deep inside the rock-face complete with brass walls and green leather seats. The notorious Martin Bormann was placed in charge of acquiring the land and the building was completed in time for Hitler's 50th birthday. After the war, the

Bavarian authorities considered blasting the place off the mountain but fortunately somebody recognised its place in history as a tourist attraction. This was a fascinating day out.

People often ask me about personal safety when travelling for a living. I have never felt threatened and surprisingly, places like New York and Chicago are safe if you are sensible. Johannesburg in South Africa was perhaps the only exception, an extremely dangerous city. We stayed in a walled compound called Sandton and never ventured out alone. The drive to the airport revealed terrible slums and an obvious high rate of unemployment. Each intersection had crowds of people standing around hoping to be picked up for day labouring jobs. Middle-class suburbs were veritable fortresses complete with razor wire, cameras and large dogs snarling through the fence. I found it a terribly depressing place. One bright spot was a restaurant called The Butcher Shop in the hotel secure compound. I have never tasted better steaks anywhere in the world.

The only incident I had while employed by Singapore Airlines was being robbed right outside the headquarters of the European Union in Brussels. I was standing still, looking up and admiring all the countries' flags fluttering outside. Two youths pulled my pullover over my head and with my arms disabled turned my back pockets inside-out. In true miserable airline captain style, there was no money in there. This was not the same for my unfortunate co-pilot who lost his wallet. He took chase after the two thieves and I yelled out to him to stop as they probably had a knife. He was sensible enough to let it go and I gave him a loan from money secure in my top pocket! We found his wallet discarded on the footpath. Empty, of course. Being young and full of vinegar, he wanted to find similar people and take them on. I had to drag him to a floor show with can-can girls to get his mind back on to more sensible activities.

American destinations were San Francisco, Los Angles, Chicago, Anchorage and New York. Sadly, as the years rolled by, San Francisco deteriorated with an increase in beggars and I no longer view it favourably. I did once give a beggar five dollars. I was walking down towards the famous Fisherman's Wharf when a Caucasian beggar suddenly popped up from inside a closed wheelie-bin. With one hand holding up the lid, the other held a sign which said, 'White Trash give generously.' Apart from scaring me witless, it made me laugh and I was only too happy to give him something. We also had quite a long chat. He was a Vietnam Vet turned alcoholic, and one could only imagine what he had been through – a true American tragedy.

Los Angeles is a monster full of concrete freeways but for me, it is a mecca for aviation museums at nearby Chino. I spent many happy hours looking at the aeroplanes of yesteryear.

Indian destinations included all their major cities, such as Mumbai, Chennai, Delhi, Calcutta and Bangalore. What can anybody say about India? (Highly polluted, chaotic traffic, chaotic airports, with unbelievable bureaucracy for just about anything.) I was once given a ticket for a city tour but it was for a full day-tour. Due to our pick-up time, I only had time for a half-day tour. "You have a blue ticket sir; you are needing a green one for a half a day" – this was said complete with head wobble. I explained that I had a ticket entitling me to a full day, but he could keep the change if I could use it for a half-day. "Oh no, sir, not possible." Nothing was ever 'possible' but I liked India simply because it was so different. There is no other place quite like it.

Australia was also covered by the roster, principally Melbourne and Sydney, but occasionally Brisbane and Perth. Overall, flying for Singapore Airlines was a fascinating experience. We worked hard, were paid well, and looked after with five-star hotels. I saw the world and went to places I would never pay a travel agency for tickets. Kuwait, for example: I never left the hotel. The Crown Plaza Hotel, where we stayed, was surrounded by a solid concrete wall designed to stop truck-bombs. Many of the guests were American 'civilian security contractors' rotating out of Iraq. They all looked like gym instructors with crew-cuts and were fascinating to talk to. I always thought flying was exciting enough but what some of these characters got up to was mind-blowing. Some were no more civilian than I am Chinese.

Unfortunately, all good things come to an end, and I gradually crept up in age, finally reaching compulsory retirement. The 747 was being slowly replaced by the new Airbus A380. I would have gone at 60 if it were not for the two-year delivery delay encountered by the Airbus A380. This enabled me to go to the new retirement age of 62. The company was kind enough to give me a special contract of three months to take me to my exact birth date. As a result, I was one of the last of the ex-pats on the fleet to leave. My last flight was my favourite Frankfurt-New York return. I was met on landing by the Human Resources Manager, complete with champagne and cake with my name emblazoned in chocolate. The deputy Fleet Manager was there and most important of all, my wife Liss. With Liss was our good friend Dr. Trish Mylan. A very emotional affair and one, a little like that first solo, I will never forget. They, too, cut my tie in half! I was also given a nice model of the 747-400 mounted on a marble block with my name and date of service. Great company to work for, they treated me well and I was sorry to leave.

16.3 Drinks on arrival, last flight 8 May 2011, Boeing 747 9V-SPO.

16.4 Operations Manager destroying my tie, 8 May 2011.

17
OUT OF RETIREMENT
2012–2022

"Why don't you come and work for us?"
Bruce Clentsmith, Manager Australian flight operations
Airwork, January 2013

I was happy to retire at 62. I was both physically and mentally tired from forty years of commercial flying. I was over living in hotels, chocolates on the pillowcase, packing a suitcase and crowded airports. I was looking forward to going back to our nice house on the Raby Bay harbour in Brisbane and doing just nothing!

It was not to be. I quickly cleaned out the garage, redecorated and painted the house and was suddenly faced with the famous 'what's next' question.

I was offered a job dropping skydivers out of a Piper Navajo by a local skydiving company. This was a typical 'low time' pilot job and I was reluctant to take away an opportunity from a young pilot climbing the ladder. On being told there was nobody else, I gave it a try. I observed a couple of drops sitting in the right-hand seat with Rodney Gin, the chief pilot, and was quickly signed off as a jump pilot.

It was great to be back flying a light-twin again but the operation was very marginal. They operated up to 15,000ft and claimed to have the highest jump height on the market. This required not only breathing oxygen (the aircraft was unpressurised) but wearing a slim-pack parachute. I enjoyed it for a while but the customers were truly crazy. One character turned up in a crocodile suit complete with a long tail.

What finally convinced me to give it away was the new winged suits that started to turn up. After a drop, I was required to get down as quickly as possible and this also required not shock-cooling the engines. I would only reduce the power by one inch of manifold pressure per each thousand feet of height loss. To keep the speed within maximum limits, the angle of bank was kept in a very steep turn with the aircraft spiralling down at a rapid rate. On one occasion the Air Traffic Controllers queried, "Confirm you are clear of your jumpers." Looking out along the wing, I was mortified to see one of these wing-suited lunatics coming down alongside the aircraft. I was also worried about these aerodynamic wing suits hitting the tail. That was enough for me; I resigned and decided this was indeed a young man's sport.

I realised that all the years of airline flying had changed me. I now preferred the disciplined standard operating procedures of multi-crew operations. I had lost my bush-pilot bravado. Gundy from my Connair days would have been horrified – I had indeed, turned into an 'airline wanker'. The good side of it was I was still alive and intended to remain so. Besides, in my opinion, passengers should be inside the aeroplane, not flying along on the outside.

I decided to renew my instructor rating and try my hand at teaching again. I accomplished this in a tiny Cessna 162 Skycatcher and it was like trying to fly a leaf! Compared to a 747 or even the Navajo light-twin, it seemed extremely sensitive to any gust loading and at times I was not sure who was flying who. My mentor was Mark Munn who calmly sat beside me while I did my best at trying to kill him. On passing the test, I was offered part-time work with Air Queensland at Redcliffe but had to find my own students. I enjoyed it for a while but the students were not plentiful. My last student I sent solo changed his mind on a fixed wing career and transitioned to helicopters. Considering my dislike of these infernal machines, this was rough justice, I suppose.

The General Aviation Industry is a far cry from my day. The industry has been crippled by red-tape, high fuel prices and the simple fact that being a pilot is no longer high on the list for young people anymore.

Not long after this brief interlude, I ran into an old acquaintance from my Ansett days. He said, "Why don't you come and work for us?" He was referring to Airwork of New Zealand. They were a company that leased aircrew and aircraft to individual customers on a contract basis. One of their contracts was TOLL, the world-wide freight forwarding company. TOLL operated six Boeing 737 freighters around Australia and the Pacific Islands. The only small print in the offer was that the position was only for a first officer slot. Many of my friends said, "Don't end your career like this." I was not fazed at all; I was never one to prance about calling myself Captain. I always remained in touch with my humble roots, and deep down I just wanted to fly for a few more years. Most of the captains at Airwork I knew from my Ansett days and some had even been my students. One Check Captain was none other than my first Instructor on joining Ansett, Pat Feeney. I accepted the offer. The warm welcome I received from Pat was a reminder of how small the aviation industry is and how the old faces keep bobbing up.

Once again, the bureaucratic pen pushers raised their ugly heads. My years on the 737 with Ansett had all been as a co-pilot on a second-class licence. Even though I had thousands of hours on type, I would have to do the whole type-rating course again!

I booked into a course with Qantas in Melbourne. Qantas made no allowances for my previous experience and I was regaled with such gems as the 'effect of speed-brakes.' "Oh, I see" became part of my vocabulary once again, but I managed not to show my frustration. I slogged away for six weeks through the soul-destroying process and regained my type rating. I have to admit I did learn a couple of new tricks. In aviation you never stop learning.

17.1 TOLL Freighters B737-400 ZK-JTQ, B737-300 ZK-FXT, Port Moresby, PNG, 24 April 2015.

So began yet another chapter in my flying career and one that turned out to the most enjoyable of all. Apart from the inter-city pairings on the night freight network, we flew right throughout the Western Pacific. Charter destinations included Vanuatu, Nauru, Tarawa, Majuro, East Timor, Manus Island, Barrow Island and Norfolk Island. Regular weekly runs were Honiara, Port Moresby, Christmas and Cocos Islands. Ground navigation aids were primitive or non-existent and it was real stick and rudder flying. It was good to feel like a pilot again and not a systems manager. I was offered extra duties as a ground instructor and began to conduct all the ground schools from initial intake to the annual refresher. The refresher was a review of all emergency systems and equipment and conducted at all the pilot bases in our network. This meant constant travel around Australia and New Zealand.

Airwork leased out aircraft to other operators and one of these was Blue Air of Romania. A ferry of one of our aircraft to Romania came up and Tim Cotter, the chief pilot, asked me to be his co-pilot for the trip. Without the endurance of a long-haul aeroplane, we flew via Darwin and Kuala Lumpur in Malaysia. After a short layover we continued via Chennai in India and Sharjah in the UAE before finally, on day three, flying into Bucharest in Romania.

During the stopover in Chennai (formerly known as Madras), Tim went off to the control tower to get the flight plan approved. I remained at the aircraft to supervise the refuelling and prepare the cockpit for departure. A very officious individual appeared out of nowhere, complete with a clipboard and wanted to see a copy of our cargo manifest. I explained to him that we were just a ferry flight and did not have one. He pointed to the pallet of ballast at the rear of the cargo hold and said that was cargo. The 737-freighter needed one ton of ballast when empty, placed in the rearmost main deck position. We used giant plastic bottles of water for this task. I explained to him that this cargo was just ballast. His demeanour immediately changed to one of great importance and he seemed to puff up and grow taller. "If it is not part of the aeroplane, it is cargo and I am wanting a manifest," he said in his broken English. "Well, we do not have one," I snapped back. He said he would get his supervisor and stomped off towards the adjacent hangar. Tim came up the stairs and said, "What was that all about?" I quickly explained and we both decided it was time to leave!

We closed the doors, obtained a start-up clearance and were soon taxying out to the runway. The take-off direction took us alongside the hanger area. On getting airborne we passed the hangar with our wheels slowly retracting into their bays only to see our manifest inspector and his supervisor standing at our previous parking spot looking skywards. Tim smiled and turning to me said, "There is one place we can't go back to."

Romania itself could only be described as 'different.' If ever proof was needed of the failures of a Communist dictatorship, it had to be Romania. Rows of bleak Soviet-style accommodation blocks lined the side of the road on the trip into town. Grass grew through the pavement and everything had a run-down appearance. The locals seemed pleasant enough but the level of inefficiency was everywhere. The most common words of English seemed to be either 'impossible' or 'problem.' Tim and I went to a local bar for a drink and met a young girl who was keen to practise her limited English. When we asked her where she was from, she replied, "I come from 18B." This was obviously one of the numbered accommodations blocks we spotted driving from the airport. A very depressing place and one I couldn't leave fast enough.

I also completed another ferry with Tim to Dothan in Alabama in the United States. It was here we had our aircraft converted into freighters. We flew an ex-Qantas 737-400 from Brisbane to Apia in Western Samoa and then planned to fly on to Kona on Big Island Hawaii. On the ground in Apia, we discovered that our 'worldwide data base' in the flight management computer did not go any further East than the Samoan Islands. We were now faced with manually loading every waypoint by latitude and longitude. This delayed us by over an hour as I laboured away entering the waypoints into the FMC. The joy of modern computers sorted, we took off and headed for Hawaii. After a short layover in Kona that had to include a swim in the sea, we flew to Long Beach in California and then direct to Dothan.

This was my first visit to the Deep South and it proved to be a very interesting trip. During the drive from the airport back to the hotel, we passed several grand-looking homes, not one having any fencing or boundary walls. On querying the driver, he said very quietly, "We don't need them, we have guns." They did indeed have guns; you could buy high calibre ammunition at the local supermarket as if it were toothpaste. It certainly was a different culture. Being a burglar in Alabama would be very exciting.

The workers in the hangar at Dothan all talked liked Gomer Pyle but were extremely friendly and accommodating. I asked one where the toilet was and just received a blank look. "I think you call it the bathroom," I said, as slowly as possible. "Y'awl mean the shitter," was the colourful reply. "Yes, old chap, that would be it," I replied. The girls in the office loved our Australian and New Zealand accents and kept asking us to engage in conversation. I found it a little embarassing, but one was obliged to try.

On the return to ferry the now converted aircraft back to New Zealand, we were delayed by a week so Tim and I hired a car and drove to Pensacola. Here we spent a day at the Naval Aviation Museum. I was in absolute heaven; their collection of aeroplanes dating back to the beginning of Naval Aviation was truly incredible. On the return to Dothan, I paid a visit to the Army Aviation Museum at Fort Rucker. For an aviation enthusiast, you could not ask for more.

After two and a half years, a new contract connecting the TOLL network to Darwin via Cairns resulted in more captain vacancies. I was selected and once again found myself in the now familiar 'meat-grinder' of ground schools and simulator. Even though I had over 20 years of experience as a captain on jet aircraft including training new captains, I was required by the Civil Aviation Authority to complete a four-day Command School. Here I re-learned such things as 'decision-making' and 'leadership' – such riveting stuff! After three months of training, I was once again back in the left-seat as a Captain. I enjoyed the flying; the trips were always interesting and included going to New Zealand and flying over there. Airwork had a joint venture with a company called Air Freight and supplied the aircraft for the New Zealand Post Office. Under the name of Parcel Air, three Boeing 737s criss-crossed the country every night.

One of the more interesting trips we flew on the Australian network was the Christmas and Cocos Islands run. Every weekend TOLL supplied a freight service to both Islands. Christmas Island contained one of three refugee camps operated by the Australian Government. Even though it was a relatively small island, Christmas was some 800 feet above sea level and had some nasty weather patterns. Around two or three times a year, the aircraft would have to divert to nearby Jakarta in Indonesia.

Christmas Island was also famous for the world's largest crab migration. Once a year the red crabs march *en masse* into the ocean to lay their eggs. It doesn't stop there, with the males then marching back inland to dig burrows for mating again with the females. The males then march off, leaving the females to care for the next batch of eggs. Prior to birth the females march back to the sea, the little crabs are born and you guessed it, they all march back inland again. So, there is a fair amount of crab traffic, to the point large signs are erected advising of road closures if the crabs were doing their thing.

Leaving Christmas Island, Cocos Island is a further one hour's flight west and we would land just before dark for a layover. Cocos also has a crab population but these are coconut crabs, so much larger. The coconut crab is a species of hermit crab and is the world's largest land-living arthropod and can weigh up to 4kg. On my first overnight there I left my motel-style room door open to savour the breeze and listen to the pounding of the surf metres away. A coconut crab decided to join me and climb up the curtains. The ensuing battle to get this brute of a thing out of the room was extensive and I discovered yet another use for old flight plans.

Manus Island was another refugee camp providing occasional charters. Located an hour's flying time north of the main island of Papua New Guinea, it was a truly remote spot. Australia would not give the people of PNG unrestricted entry into Australia and required a visa. Understandably, the PNG Government in retaliation required Australian citizens to also acquire a visa. This could take up to six weeks. There were no restrictions on most other nationalities where a short-term visa was available on arrival.

17.2 Final approach, Cocos Island, 6 November 2015.

17.3 George Palmer, and remains of war memorial on Manus Island, Momote, PNG, 13 January 2017.

With my dual citizenship, when a charter to Manus came up, I was a regularly assigned pilot. I would leave Australia on an Australian passport and morph into an Englishman en route. Arriving in Port Moresby on an English passport I would overnight on their short-stay visa. I would then travel as an Englishman from Port Moresby to Manus Island and return the next morning.

We would leave very early in the morning from Jackson Field, just after daybreak as Manus Island aerodrome had no serviceable navigation aids. The aim was to get in and out before the afternoon rain showers formed. We were always accompanied by a ground-engineer, complete with a spares kit to prevent being trapped by a break-down. Climbing out of Port Moresby, we would cross the rugged mountain range running along the spine of the country with minimum safe altitudes of over 17,000 feet. Single-engine performance at high weights had to be considered but we were normally restricted by the maximum landing weight at Manus. Once over the 'other side', we would let down to our minimum safe altitude and look for a break in the clouds.

I enjoyed this type of flying but it required great care. We would overfly the aerodrome and check the wind direction from the windsock just like a big Cessna and then fly a tight circuit. The runway itself was long enough but not very even. It was like riding a horse bouncing along to a halt – bush flying in a jet!

During the unloading I often walked to the nearby lagoon and here several reminders of the island's history still remained. Radial engines and airframe parts including a wing were to be found in the shallows; all remnants of the Second World War.

Manus is an interesting place and very beautiful. If you had to be locked up by the Australian Government in the nearby detention centre, you couldn't complain about the scenery. On the way home to Brisbane, I would once again regain my Australian nationality. I still worry about a computer somewhere in England recording one of their citizens leaving and arriving from nowhere to visit an Australian Detention Centre.

Chris Hanna, the Training Manager at the time, asked me if I would like to be a Training Captain. I readily agreed. Unlike my Ansett days where it was only a two-day instructor's course, the New Zealanders were *War and Peace*. I had to complete a five-day Instructional Technique course with Air New Zealand followed by simulators and briefing exercises. The simulator test itself was over four hours with the examiner being 'an awkward student,' a task he accomplished surprisingly well. This was followed by observation flights, observing other instructors 'instructing' and finally three sectors with an examiner flying from the right-hand seat. Needless to say, my previous eight years of instructing on 727s and 747s was completely ignored. By now I had a degree with honours in 'the right attitude', and passed the course still smiling, and obtained what the Kiwis call a Cat-D. I have always enjoyed training and began training new pilots both on the ground and in the air.

A favourite for me when training was to get our new pilots out into the Pacific islands and away from the big city airports. One of our weekly services was to Honiara in the Solomon Islands. The airport at Guadalcanal was where the Americans finally stopped the Japanese and turned the bitter conflict around. The main island runs east-west with a high mountain range to the south running along the entire length. The cloud tended to sit over the mountains and we would commence a 'step-down' type of approach and invariably break out in clear skies right over the airfield. We would then join the circuit and descend further to 1500ft. Thick jungle covered the mountains but the flat coastal plains were covered in plantations. The ridges around the southern aerodrome perimeter looked unnaturally chopped up with gullies and round depressions going in all directions. Similar to the fields of Flanders, this was overgrown shell holes. Once you realised what you were looking at, especially from the air, it gave true scale to the conflicts of the past. Half-sunken vessels still dot the coconut-lined beaches.

Overnights were very pleasant affairs – warm still nights without a breath of wind and seas like glass. There is something unique about a tropical night. It's truly peaceful watching the lightning flashing on the horizon and having a cool beer with a fellow flyer.

17.4 Unloading B737-400 ZK-TLJ, Honiara, Solomon Islands, 27 July 2017.

The only new problem coming my way was my age. I was now over 65 and no longer allowed in French Airspace. On a trip to Vanuatu, the flight plan nominated Noumea as an alternate and I queried this with Ops. "Don't worry; you will not end up there, the weather is fine," they said, but it was obvious the writing was on the wall. I had visions of being jailed by the French and sent to Devil's Island in chains. I continued flying overseas to the age of 68, mainly around the Pacific Islands but finally the Australian Civil Aviation Safety Authority stepped in and told the company that only pilots under 65 could fly internationally. There is no age limit for flying in Australia and New Zealand domestically. Restricted to the rather dull domestic night roster, I accepted an offer to be the Line Operations Manager.

I now began a pattern of flying and office work. I enjoyed this but the managerial side could be stressful at times, dealing with the personal problems that seem to surround the pilot population. Apart from the usual union disputes over rostering and contractual grievances, many of the pilots had terrible family problems. Divorce was common but also such issues such as children with a disability and financial stress. I considered most of the pilots to be personal friends and had known some of them for over forty years. It was a difficult job trying to help them and also have the company's interest at heart. 'Running with the foxes and hunting with the hounds' readily comes to mind.

I was promoted further to the position of Deputy Flight Manager of Flight Operations referred to by the acronym-loving industry as the DFMO. Together with my training commitments, both on the ground and in the air, I began to experience a level of fatigue similar to long-haul flying. Now rapidly approaching 70, I decided to give it away and once again retired. My last flight out of Australia was a ferry flight to Singapore where the company scheduled deep maintenance or what was called a C-Check. Even though I had attained the age of 69, it was permitted by operating as a private flight under Part 91 of the NZ CAA regulations. My co-pilot was Sebastian Murray who was about to start his command upgrade. Seb was a good friend and came from a flying family, with a brother flying F/A-18 Hornets in the RAAF. He also owned a Piper Cub light-aircraft and it was a pleasure to pass the baton to such a capable character.

Having filed a flight plan as a Private Flight, I told Seb it might be wise to take extra fuel. Being at the bottom of air traffic priorities, I expected holding delays. To our surprise we were given direct to everywhere with no delays and even track shortening. I think they thought we were some sort of millionaires with our own private jet and just wanted us out of the way.

My last week was spent over in New Zealand finishing the training of our first female pilot, Clare Drinkwater. Clare was also very young and very capable and further proof that people of my age should know when to hand over the reins. The industry is in very safe hands.

My last flight, by a strange coincidence, was the same place I first flew a jet, Christchurch, New Zealand. Not only that, but it was also the same type – a 737! The Airport Fire Section formed a water arch as I taxied onto the cargo ramp. On arriving back in Auckland on a domestic flight, I was met by all the duty staff for tea and sandwiches. Once again, I was presented with a chocolate cake! I felt like an imposter going through the same ritual as in Singapore.

I was offered the opportunity to stay involved with the company as a Ground Instructor/Simulator Instructor and this leads us to the present. One of the simulators the company uses is the old Ansett 737-300 simulator in Melbourne. This is the very one in which I was subjected to various levels of torture back in the early eighties. It is a strange feeling being on the other end of the stick, programming disasters for the anxious trainees.

Most of our full-flight simulator sessions are conducted with Qantas at their Simulator Centre in Essendon. Here I have many reunions with former Ansett pilots now flying for Jetstar and Qantas. Many of my old co-pilots now hold management positions and the new Qantas second officers look like teenagers. It is remarkable to think where fifty years have gone. At least I am contributing in some way helping the new generation but the awful feeling of being 'yesterday's hero' persists. On the bright side, I feel I have some empathy towards my students, able to understand what they are going through and it is very satisfying seeing them released to the sky.

18
COVID
2020–2022

> *"Finally, something out of China that lasts more than six months."*
> Letter to editor local newspaper, Brisbane

On 25 January 2020 in Melbourne, Victoria, the first case of COVID-19 was detected. The patient, from Wuhan in China, had arrived in Australia via Guangdong on 19 January. The rest, as they say is history. At the time of writing, over 4 million people worldwide have died including over 900 in Australia. One thousand people a day were dying in America, and there were similar figures in Europe.

The effect on the aviation industry has been nothing short of catastrophic. Virgin Airlines went into bankruptcy almost immediately, although many argue it was heading down that path anyway. Qantas virtually ceased all international services and reduced domestic runs to a trickle. Hundreds of pilots were laid off, accepted leave without pay, or full redundancy. Throughout the world, a similar picture began to emerge. Aircraft storage parks quickly filled up and the industry virtually ground to a halt. Qantas captains were driving farm machinery and even washing cars. This was tragic; everyone hoped things would recover soon.

Despite China hiding the truth and refusing to accept any responsibility, anybody who has visited a Chinese wet market can readily suspect the origins of a pandemic. They are truly awful places and not for the faint-hearted, especially anyone who has a soft spot for animals. The world of cargo flying, however not only survived but actually picked up extra freight normally carried by the passenger aircraft in their underfloor holds.

Airwork quickly obtained further contracts including a Tasman crossing for Fed-Ex. New pilots were recruited and I was asked to help complete the type-ratings in the simulator in Melbourne. One of the new recruits was Arthur Jackson who had flown Jaguars and Tornados in the RAF. We met during my skydiving days and became good friends. Due to COVID-19 restrictions, we were more or less imprisoned in our Melbourne serviced apartments. A difficult endorsement program but to Arthur and his simulator partner Jason Leonard's credit, they both made easy work of it. Arthur, on leaving the RAF, flew as a military instructor with the Royal Saudi Air Force. He next flew as a Captain on a Westwind jet completing aero medical evacuation duties based in Malaysia. His main difficulty was being away from his family for weeks at a time. Even though the Airwork position was only for a First Officer position, Arthur was only too glad to accept it and spend more time with his family. Jason was a typical young general aviation pilot but was unusual in that he had been living in France. After marrying a French girl and learning the language, he returned to Australia. It was always a pleasure to work with such interesting and capable characters and we had an enjoyable time.

Where to from here? I have rekindled my interest in light aircraft and upgraded my Grade 2 Instructor Rating on my Australian licence to a Grade 1. More study, of course, and a short period of dual instruction of five hours followed by a flight test. I intend to teach both in the simulator for Airwork and instruct in light aircraft. The medical requirements will eventually be my decider. At 72 my right ear is down 33 decibels, the limit being 35 before a hearing aid. So, I guess eventually I will have to hang up the wings one day. Flying to me is not a job, it is a way of life; the sense of freedom to soar with the birds has never left me. I have spent my working life looking forward to going to work. It is such a shame that the bureaucrats continue to bog down all aspects of the industry, reinventing the wheel at every turn.

A recent example of bureaucracy gone mad was renewing my airport security card. Despite the fact I have been on their books for over fifty years, the whole exercise was as if it were for initial issue. Birth certificate, pilot's licence, citizen certificate and even a rates notice! This was followed up by a personal interview to verify I am who I say I am, complete with all the documentation once again. I told them I had a letter from the Pope as well, but it didn't draw a smile. All were very serious.

A good friend doing contract flying in Asia once said, "You have to have two buckets, one for the money and one for the bullshit, whichever one fills up first, and you go home." One of my buckets filled up many years ago and it was not the money one. I have just learnt to keep my opinions to myself. After all, think of those poor devils working in an office from nine to five, all their working lives. They will never know what they have missed. They can do what they like – I feel I am so far in front they will never wear me down.

APPENDIX A
THE BRISTOL B170 FREIGHTER

The Bristol was the first pure heavy freighter to enter Australian service after World War II. It was a product of the famous English firm, the Bristol Aeroplane Company Limited of Filton. The British army issued a specification for a freighter that could carry one of its three-ton trucks and it was initially designed around this requirement. The first prototype flew on 2 December 1945. After a few modifications, including lowering the tailplane, the aircraft was placed into production. The British Army in the end failed to order any after setting the basic design parameters. Several Air Forces around the world did place orders, the largest was by the Pakistan Air Force which ordered no fewer than 35 Mk21P and 38 Mk31M freighters.

The RAAF received four Mk21E freighters principally to support the testing grounds at Woomera. I flew one of these, as well as one previously owned by the Pakistan Air Force.

The Australian connection to the aircraft started in an almost comical fashion. A Mk1A demonstrator flew out for a sales tour on 20 March 1947. After landing at Wau in New Guinea on 23 November, the crew disembarked on the steeply sloping airfield only to see the aircraft slowly rolling backwards downhill. Although the parking brake had been applied, it either couldn't hold the weight or had failed. The sales team had the unpleasant experience of watching the aircraft wreck itself at the bottom of the airstrip.

Nevertheless, several Australian operators did order the aircraft and it proved successful in its specialist role. Australian National Airways used them on what was called The Air Beef Scheme. Instead of moving cattle vast distances in the remote areas of Australia by drovers, an abattoir was established inland and the frozen beef flown to the coastal city regions. Three Bristols were used for this flying, all three eventually flying for Ansett Airlines. Other operators in Australia include Jet Airways and Trans Australian Airlines (TAA). The final operator was Air Express Ltd of Essendon Melbourne (flown by me).

A description of what they were like to fly has been covered adequately in the main narrative, but a few further points may be of interest. The aircraft had a disturbing history of losing a wing in flight. The Bristol was designed before modern 'fail-safe' principles and was built with a single rigid spar. One of the four RAAF examples (A81-2) lost a wing near Mallala in South Australia a day before I was born, on 13 May 1949. On descent passing 5,000ft, the left wing failed outboard of the engine nacelle. The aircraft rolled over and came down in a wheat field killing the three crew. It was suspected the aircraft had been previously overstressed as the weather at the time was fine. Another Bristol in New Zealand, ZK-AYH, operated by Straits Air Freight Express also crashed after the right wing separated on 21 November 1957.

Armed with this history, when flying with Air Express I was always fascinated by watching in flight, a crease in the leading edge moving slowly towards the wing tip only to see it slowly working its way back again. Not being pressurised, the aircraft's 'life' was based on the number of landings and Air Express flew all their aircraft to the end of their useful life. Happily, the wings remained firmly in place. It was always in the back of my mind – not that you could do much about it.

Two Bristols remain in Australia as static exhibits, one Mk21E (Ex VH-SJG) at the RAAF Base Museum Point Cook and a Mk31 at Moorabbin Airport (ex VH-ADL). There are several in New Zealand, including one used as a bed and breakfast!

APPENDIX B
THE DE HAVILLAND DH114 HERON

First flown on 10 May 1950, the De Havilland DH114 Heron was a four-engine development of the successful De Havilland Dove. Unlike the Dove, the initial Mk 1 model was unusual in that it was designed with a fixed undercarriage. The idea was to create a simple-to-maintain rugged feeder liner that could operate off unprepared strips. Together with Gypsy Queen Engines, the aircraft proved to be a poor performer. Only 51 of the fixed undercarriage versions were built. The Mk 2 quickly followed with a more sensible retractable undercarriage and first flew on 14 December 1952. Only 97 aircraft of this version were built, so in pure numbers, the aircraft could be considered a commercial failure. This is not entirely true as some operators found them, in the right market, a valuable asset. One American operator, Prinair, acquired no fewer than 25 of them.

The low-powered gypsy engines continued to be the aircraft's biggest drawback. It was inevitable that someone would come up with an alternative engine and the Mexican company Vest Aircraft de Mexico SA did just that. The modified aircraft was fitted with four 340hp Lycoming GSO-480 engines, and the change in performance was remarkable. An American engineer, Jack Riley, was not keen on the temperamental geared engines and settled on a more modest conversion to the Lycoming IO-540 of 290 hp. This became almost the standard conversion with FAA approval gained on 3 March 1962.

The first Australian operator of Herons was Butler Air transport placing a Mk1B into service on 4 November 1952. This was used to fly passengers on a schedule Sydney to Temora and return three times a week. This was followed by a second aircraft and both proved to be popular with the travelling public, many preferring them to the larger DC3. The Butler Herons were equipped to carry a crew of 2 and 14 passengers and came with a toilet. The fixed undercarriage of the Mk1 in Butler service actually proved its worth with some of the mud found on the unprepared strips in NSW.

The first Heron for the Northern territory Airline Connellan Airways (later renamed Connair and finally Northern airlines) were delivered in March 1963. Mk2s with retractable undercarriages, they were equipped with the original Gypsy Queen engines. As with previous operators, Connellan also found them underpowered especially in the heat at Alice Springs. The company converted them to Riley Herons in-house. The first aircraft modified was VH-CLT in 1969 at a cost of $100,000 and 2,000 work-hours. Connair eventually purchased 9 Herons but only flew 7 at any given time. The aircraft played a major role in developing tourism in the Northern Territory and proved a great success.

Unfortunately, Connair suffered a fatal accident with the Heron on 23 October 1975. After commencing an instrument approach (ILS) to Cairns on runway 15, the aircraft failed to align correctly and commenced a missed approach. In very heavy rain and with a thunderstorm in the area, the crew failed to follow the published procedure and attempted to remain visual in a low-level manoeuvre. The aircraft struck treetops while in a forty-degree bank turn and crashed into a cane field short of the runway. The reason for this manoeuvre was to remain unknown, the aircraft was not fitted with a cockpit voice recorder or a flight data recorder. The pilot in command had relatively low Instrument Flying time and only 87 hours at night. It is possible he reverted to where he felt more comfortable but with fatal results. Three crew members and eight passengers were killed. Following this accident, Connair adopted rigid airline style Standard Operating Procedures (SOPs).

What were they like to fly? As previously stated in the manuscript the cockpit was small and cramped, noisy and hot in the high temperatures of Northern Australia. The propellers needed constant attention to keep them in sync via electrical switches and a series of blue lights. Pneumatics was the order of the day for brakes and flaps. The flaps themselves were fabric-covered and very large, giving a steep approach. The primary flight controls were all cable-driven and manual but even still, the aircraft was not unusually heavy in 'feel'. The ailerons were also fabric-covered, and this no doubt helped. The aircraft was surprisingly clean aerodynamically and required planning ahead on descent and was difficult to slow down. Easy to land and seemed to settle itself gently onto the main undercarriage without too much pilot input. Water seeping into the electrical and radio compartment was always a problem. The radios were installed in the nose cone which required constant use of tape to keep the water out. Overall, a pleasant enough aeroplane to fly but at the time I did not enjoy it much. A progressive load sheet was one problem which required some concentration to keep it running among multiple sectors.

One amusing incident demonstrated crew resourcefulness that was hard to beat. Faced with an unruly full load of passengers, the captain tied a small teddy bear around a length of tape. Opening the small storm window in the cockpit (the Heron was not pressurised) he slowly released the bundled-up tape and allowed the slipstream to 'walk' the toy bear along the outside of the window line. The superstitious locals became instant model passengers staring wide-eyed straight ahead as the toy bear slid past. It was not unusual to lose a passenger on a turn-around, they would simply walk off into the bush. Sometimes they would spot a relative and disappear. 'Jimmy Wednesday' became a common fix to fill in a missing space on the manifest and balance the books!

APPENDIX C
THE FOKKER F27 FRIENDSHIP

Following World War II, several aircraft manufactures set about designing and building a Douglas DC-3 replacement. It could be said that nobody really achieved this. Over 16,000 DC-3s and the military version C47 were built. Even today some 200 are still flying. One aircraft that could claim this title, if numbers built are ignored, is the Fokker F27. Australia enjoyed great success with this aircraft, and it was widely used over secondary and regional routes.

First flown on 24 November 1955 the initial orders were for six aircraft for Trans Australian Airlines (TAA) at a cost of £1.2 million. Subsequent orders increased the type on the Australian register to no fewer than 81. Ansett through its various subsidiaries can claim to be the biggest operator of the type.

The aircraft was popular with the public, offering a comfortable pressurised cabin with large oval windows beneath a high set wing. Unfortunately, the aircraft had a poor start with a fatal accident on 10 June 1960. A F27-100 of TAA, VH-TFB flew into the sea while making a night approach in fog to Mackay. All 29 occupants were killed. With no cockpit voice recorder or flight data recorder, the cause was never fully determined. It was at night, in poor visibility, with optical illusions over the sea being a prime suspect. It must be remembered these were the days before sophisticated navigational aids were available.

On 31 May 1974, East West Airlines lost a F27 at Bathurst in NSW, fortunately without injury to the 30 passengers and four crew. The aircraft suffered a sudden change in wind from a 30-knot headwind to a 30-knot tailwind while on late final approach. During an attempted missed approach, the aircraft failed to climb away. It is believed this unusual event was the result of a micro-burst, a phenomenon not fully understood at the time. Micro-bursts are very localised but extremely powerful downdrafts emanating out of the bottom of large storm clouds.

From the crew viewpoint there are some who loved the aircraft, but others were at best, indifferent. In Ansett service, it was considered by many to be only a stepping-stone to the coveted jets. As a result, many Ansett pilots would only fly it for a few years. The cockpit was cramped and noisy with the two Rolls-Royce Dart engines giving out a high-pitched howl that gave way to the nickname 'the twenty-ton dog whistle'. Engine handling and propeller controls were complicated, and the pressurisation required constant manual adjustment. Fuel trimmers, as described in the main text, also required constant adjustment via spring-loaded switches to the rear of the centre console. In addition, water methanol was used for high power requirements described as wet-power and introduced via overhead switches. It seemed to be an unnecessarily busy aircraft, but I still enjoyed my time on the type.

It took me over a year to fully understand the propeller with its various locks. Ansett even lost one aircraft due to a propeller lock fault. On 17 March 1965, VH-FNH was on approach to Launceston. With the left engine shut down as a direct result of a propeller lock failure, the crew lost directional control on late approach to Runway 32. Simply put, they got behind the drag curve with landing flaps at 40 degrees and lost control. While the aircraft was written off, the 23 occupants escaped injury. Single-engine approach procedures were subsequently changed to restrict flap to 26.5 degrees maximum for approach. TAA had a similar loss of control on 9 June

1982 while crew training at Amberley in Queensland. With the left engine shut down, directional control was lost on applying power to the remaining engine. Again, no injuries but the aircraft was damaged beyond economical repair. This was the last accident to a F27 in Australian service. In 1987, Ansett F27s was replaced with the Fokker F50.

APPENDIX D
THE BOEING 727

The Boeing 727 is the aircraft that introduced many countries to jet travel – Australia was one of them. Both Ansett and TAA ordered the aircraft and first deliveries of the 100-version arrived in Melbourne on 16 October 1964. What followed was a long and successful career with the two carriers. Ansett finally retired the type in April 1997. In terms of numbers built, only 1832 727s were manufactured compared to the over 15,500 737s of all models. It is considered by many to be a cornerstone in jet airliner design and remembered fondly by all who operated and maintained them.

The aircraft was fast and even looked fast when parked on the ground. In aviation they say, "If it looks right, it will fly right" and never was a truer word spoken when it came to this iconic aeroplane. Like all beautiful thoroughbreds, it could bite if mishandled and demanded attention to detail, especially close to the ground. Speed and sink control were essential to achieve a good landing. The greatest sin was to be slow with a high sink rate, throw in flap 40 and a crosswind and life could get very exciting very quickly. Once mastered, the smoothest landings of one's career were possible, until you relaxed again!

As mentioned in the text, Ansett was unique in ordering the long-range version, the -200LR. Only four were delivered, the first,

VH-ANA on 16 June 1981. This was followed by ANB, ANE and ANF. 'F' for Foxtrot was one of those aeroplanes that exhibited its own personality, needing constant trimming of the rudder. It quickly gained the nickname, the Crab, and no cause of this abnormality was ever discovered – general opinion believed it was completed on a late Friday afternoon before a long weekend. I thought the straight 200 was nicer to fly, as the LR was several tons heavier with the same available thrust and could be sluggish on a hot day. Ansett ordered the LR with the -15 engines, and with the luxury of hindsight, the more powerful -17 engines would have been the ideal combination.

For the passengers it had to be one of the most comfortable rides available, especially up the front. Quiet and a good stable aeroplane in turbulence, it was hard to beat. I have heard that the British VC-10 was similar but unfortunately, I have never flown in one. What killed the 727 was fuel consumption. They were known as the Cadillac of the skies and unfortunately, they burnt fuel like their namesake. Fuel usage was around 10,000 lbs or 5 tons an hour on the three engines. They just could not compete with the modern high by-pass twin engine aircraft that began to appear. For those of us who flew them, nobody can take away the memories. We were very lucky indeed.

APPENDIX E
THE BOEING 737

The original model Boeing 737-100 first flew on 9 April 1967. The first customer was Lufthansa of Germany. Over the years, the basic design has continued to grow with increased capacity and power to the problematic Max series of today. Ansett was the first Australian airline to order the type, placing an order for 12 737-200AV (advanced). The first, VH-CZM, was delivered on 20 June 1981. They were only to be in service for six years before being replaced by the larger 300 version in 1986. At the time of their introduction, the B737 was hailed as the first of the new computerised jets. Considering the modern computerised aircraft of today, this claim now seems laughable, but they were a big step forward in automation, with a full flight regime auto throttle, together with a Performance Data Computer System (PDCS) and VLF Omega navigation system. Their relatively short life was dictated by rising fuel prices, the JT-8-15 engines being thirsty, not to mention very noisy as well.

On 2 August 1986, the first of the new 300 version were delivered. Stretched with modern high-bypass turbofan engines (CFM-56), they offered considerable fuel savings and were to remain in service until Ansett's demise. The first of the 300s was VH-CZA, which I flew in Ansett only to run into the aircraft 25 years later to fly it again with Airwork of NZ. The aircraft eventually went to Blue Air in Romania where presumably it has ended its days peacefully.

The 737 was not the nicest of the Boeings to fly. It is short-coupled and overly sensitive in pitch. The underslung engines cause a nose-up pitch with any increase in thrust and vice versa. The 200, in my opinion, was too light in roll and it was easy to overcontrol. If you had to pick a Boeing for a dogfight the 200 was the machine, but not a feature required for flying the general public about. The 300 was much heavier in roll control and felt about right.

TAA/Australian Airlines went a step further and ordered the 400 version. A further stretch with a further power increase, these aircraft would eventually become part of Qantas. Five of these aircraft would be bought by Airwork and converted into freighters, and all were flown by me. Under the Two Airline Policy I would often taxi out behind the opposition's 400 series, if somebody had said, "One day you will be flying that," I would have thought, never in a million years. Aviation is like that; you never know what is around the corner!

The 400 was definitely the nicest of the 737s to fly, especially in landings. It was possible to mess up a landing, but you had to work at it. Once in the flare, the aircraft seemed to settle gracefully on its own and touch down smoothly. A real lady, providing you did not do too much of that piloting business. Just leave it alone, with gentle guidance and it landed beautifully. A quarterly crosswind/tailwind required more attention with a tendency to float if you tried too hard for a smooth landing. Overall, it was a nice handling aeroplane, close to the ground.

Where people got themselves into trouble on the 737 was full-rated power go-arounds. The aircraft would quickly get out of trim and some pilots failed to understand the power of the all-moving tailplane and the importance of not trimming to stick position. With a fixed elevator, you trim to stick or control column position but with an all-moving tailplane it was important to trim to a neutral position. The elevator and the control column that moved it was only around 25 per cent of pitch authority. The rest, from the powerful electric/hydraulic tailplane or stabiliser, actuated via a trim switch on the control wheel. Some nasty loss of control accidents overseas has sadly proved this point. To me, this stresses the vital importance of good training. Take short cuts at your peril – something accountants have trouble understanding.

As a freighter, the aircraft is operating in an environment it was never designed for. Empty, it requires a ton of ballast in the rearmost position. The cargo door itself comes in several versions depending on the source of the conversion. Airwork had mainly the AEI (Aircraft Engineers Inc.) cargo door manufactured in Dothan Alabama. The large bulge on the top hinge has a slight yaw effect and the aircraft requires one degree of left rudder trim to fly straight. The 300 has nine bays or main deck positions and the 400 has 11. With a freight capacity of 20 tons, it has proven its worth and been a commercial success.

APPENDIX F
THE BOEING 747

Much has been written about this aircraft and there is no doubt history will record it as a significant development up there alongside the DC-3. The Jumbo brought long distance travel to people who could never previously afford it and opened the world to mass tourism. To some, overshadowed by the A380 but to most, still the queen of the skies.

First flight of the prototype was on 9 February 1969 and the aircraft entered service with Pan American World Airways on 21 January the following year. Like all modern jet aircraft, the basic model changed considerably over the following 20 years. Perhaps the biggest change came in 1989 with the launch of the 400 series. Gone was the Flight Engineer and round dials, to be replaced with a two-pilot 'glass cockpit' with CRT screens and a high level of automation. This has been replaced with an even more efficient 800 series with a new wing and redesigned flap layout, not to mention an increase in length and weight. During 2022, the aircraft was still in limited production some 50 years from the first flight, albeit mainly in cargo variants.

The first 747 in Australia was naturally delivered to Qantas, as the sole Australian International carrier at the time. On 16 August 1971, VH-EBA, a B747-200B 'City of Canberra' touched down in

Sydney. So began a long career with Qantas with this type that would last over 50 years. Qantas ordered the -200, 200 Combi (a mix of passengers and freight), the SP (Special Performance), the 300, 400 and finally the 400 ER for extended range. Ansett leased three 300s from Singapore Airlines in 1994 followed by two 400s. It should be noted that Ansett also operated several American-registered Singapore 747s when its own aircraft were down for maintenance. At one stage, even a Malaysia Airlines aircraft was substituted.

I flew the 300 and 400 with Ansett and the 300, 300 Combi, 400 and 400F (freighter) with Singapore Airlines. What were they like to fly? In some ways, the easiest of the Boeings but they did require more flight management especially in fuel. The 400 version had over 170 tons of useable fuel in eight tanks. Unlike surface transport, there are too many variables in aviation to talk of precise fuel rates but suffice to say it was around ten tons an hour. With a maximum take-off weight of 398,000kg and a maximum landing weight of 285,000kg (302,000kg on the freighter) the aircraft had a very efficient fuel dumping system.

The aircraft was fast by commercial jet standards with a cruise speed around .86 Mach number. Designed as a long-haul aeroplane, it was no rocket in take-off performance at high weights and high temperatures. Taking off at maximum weight in the hot humid air at Changi in Singapore for Europe, the aircraft was slow to accelerate and used most of the long runway. Reaching Vr (rotate speed) a slow 2 to 3-degree rate of rotation resulted in a gentle departure from the earth with vapour vortices emanating off the leading-edge flaps. The engine intakes also filled with a thick mist in the humidity. It felt heavy and vulnerable as it initially climbed away with the undercarriage retracting. Initial flap retraction from take-off flap 20 could only be made with the wings level. To do so in a banked turn caused the high and low speed buffet boundaries on the speed tape to ominously start to merge. Maximum altitude at these weights was in the high twenties – it took four hours and somewhere over India before we could get above 30,000 feet.

When the A380 first appeared, the one thing that struck me was they had no such performance restrictions and climbed straight away to 30,000 feet. Where the 747 came into its own was a few hours into the cruise, it seemed to find its step and charge off towards the destination like a racehorse. Even though we had fuel heaters, cold fuel was often a problem and to avoid ice in the fuel we had to descend into warmer air or go faster where the skin friction literally warmed the fuel.

January 2008 was a particularly cold winter and one night over Warsaw the outside temperature was -64 degrees Celsius. Everybody was asking to get down into warmer air with cold fuel issues. All levels below us were blocked so I went to Mach .88 to keep the fuel within limits. If you couldn't get down, going faster literally warmed up the tanks a few degrees by skin friction.

One aircraft, a British Airways 777 on a flight from Beijing to London (BA38) was behind us all night and didn't seem to have any problems. However, while landing, both engines failed to respond to thrust lever movement. They touched down heavily short of the runway, luckily with no serious injuries but writing the aeroplane off. Watching the news from the edge of my hotel bed in London that morning, I said to myself, "That will be fuel ice." Two years later after the investigation was finally completed, fuel ice was the culprit. All they had to do was ask the crews flying that night. To be fair to the crew of BA38, a poor design feature in the fuel filters themselves was the cause of the blockage. The filters were subsequently modified.

Landing weights after a long flight to Europe were around 240,000kg which resulted in an Approach reference speed in the region of 140 knots. At these weights and speeds the aeroplane was highly manoeuvrable and easy to fly. A great aeroplane and loved by all who flew it. Perhaps the only criticism, the cockpit was small and cramped for an aircraft of its size. Also, there were no cockpit windows that could be opened on the ground. In the Middle East without air conditioning, it could be unbearably hot, and we would open the overhead cockpit escape hatch to get some fresh air. The 15 years I spent as a 747 Captain were the highlight of my career. Having said that, I do not miss long-haul flying. Once you stop this type of flying, the level of fatigue you have become accustomed to then becomes apparent. The long-term detrimental effects on your health cannot be ignored.

APPENDIX G
THE GAF NOMAD

This was probably the most controversial aeroplane manufactured in this country since World War II, but was it really that bad? Some misinformation and bad publicity have followed this aircraft and there is no doubt it had some design faults. In my mind, it was another lost opportunity for the Australian aviation industry. With some modifications the Nomad had great potential.

The prototype first flew on 23 July 1971 and after 172 were built, production ceased in 1985. Two principal variants were built; the N22 and the stretched N24. Various sub-variants were built according to task requirements such as coastal surveillance. Over 30 hull losses were recorded during its peak. With less than a handful flying today, the aircraft is remembered as a failure. Removing all the hysteria and emotion so favoured by the press, many of these accidents proved no fault of the aeroplane. The aeroplane had to be loaded correctly and several accidents were caused by the aircraft being outside its centre of gravity limits.

On 6 June 1976, 11 people were killed in an accident, including the Chief Minister for Sabah Malaysia, following an approach into Kota Kinabalu Malaysia. The investigation showed the aircraft was incorrectly loaded, including being overloaded in the rear locker. Conducting a low-level orbit at low speed to allow spacing with other traffic, the aircraft stalled and spun into the sea. Due to the high profile of the occupants, Malaysia has never fully released its findings. All sorts of conspiracy theories began to circulate through the industry. The Australian investigation concluded pilot error coupled with an aft centre of gravity caused the loss of control at a height too low for recovery. Overloading any aircraft raises the stall speed and any aeroplane with an aft centre of gravity becomes unstable in pitch. Get slow in a turn and the results are predictable.

One known weakness was in the design of the tail and there are two recorded instances of tailplane failure. On reading the reports there is more to these accidents than what meets the eye. On 12 March 1990, a RAAF Nomad lost its tail and crashed near Mallala in South Australia, and the pilot was killed on impact. The subsequent investigation revealed the aircraft had been used by the Aircraft Research and Development Unit (ARDU) for single-engine ground running tests for no less than 177 hours. Due to the abnormal amount of asymmetrical torsional loading on the tail from the propeller wash, fatigue cracks had developed. Under normal flight loads the tailplane finally failed. The aircraft was never designed to be run on the ground on one engine for endless hours at a time.

The other case was an accident in Indonesia where the wreck was discovered minus the tail. With the harsh operating environment in that part of the world, coupled with dubious maintenance standards, that case remains open. The tailplane problems could have been easily fixed and indeed at the time production ended, an airframe with a modified T-Tail was being evaluated.

The other problem was the choice of the engine. The little Allison 250 B17 engines of 420 shp were very economical but in hot weather the aircraft was underpowered. Temperature limits were reached before torque limits, giving only modest performance. Engine ice ingestion was a problem in the early days but solved with a clever redesign of the engine cowl.

Other peculiar problems included rain or surface water shorting out a micro-switch on the rear door. This switch prevented the flaps from being lowered as they were within the arc of an open door. With water running off the top surface of the wing onto the door lip, the switch would be affected and prevent lowering of the flaps. Operating off unprepared strips, mud would gather inside the undercarriage pods and jam the gear doors which folded up inside the pods with the gear down. The simple solution, taken by most operators, was to simply remove the undercarriage doors.

From a pilot's perspective, it did have some unpleasant roll forces especially with full flap down but nothing that could be deemed dangerous. The aeroplane was a capable machine if operated safely within its design envelope. I enjoyed flying them and some spectacular short landings could be accomplished once you gained some experience on type. 'Death Trap Nomads' was the title written by one journalist in the *Herald Sun* on 27 January 2004. Military pilots claimed the aircraft were unsafe and called them 'the widow maker'. In the time I flew them I never had a problem apart from the chip detector issue as described in the main text. With some redesign the aircraft could have been a real winner. There is a tendency to knock anything locally produced and, in this instance, I feel it was unfairly demonised.

APPENDIX H
LIGHT AIRCRAFT

Light aircraft are a difficult summary because I have been fortunate to fly a variety of all the major types. American aircraft feature prominently, being the largest manufacturers. Three companies dominate the market – Beechcraft, Piper and Cessna, all American. The industry has suffered over the years due to public liability insurance issues and the market is only producing a fraction of the aircraft compared to the industry heydays of the mid-seventies and eighties. Cessna once had a wide range of light piston twins and now only produces single-engine piston aircraft.

The only British-built light aircraft I flew were the DH82 Tiger Moth, DHC-1 Chipmunk, Britten-Norman Islander and the Auster. The Chipmunk is a Canadian design built in the UK. Interesting to reflect that the nicest handling single is the Chipmunk and the worst is the Auster! The Auster is a 'tail dragger' but has such oddities as heel brakes instead of the more common toe brakes, a ceiling mounted trim wheel that gloriously works the opposite way to American aircraft. Indeed, even the engine rotates the opposite way to American designs, requiring a touch of left rudder on take-off instead of the more common right for directional control. None of these are a showstopper but the straw that breaks the camel's back is the tendency to bounce about on landing. The only way to land with any sense of dignity is to kill all lift in a three-point attitude at the point of a stall. The Chipmunk has beautifully balanced and harmonised controls and will fly itself along quite happily without any tendency to wander off.

Out of the American singles nothing can beat a Beechcraft Bonanza. Solidly built and well-engineered, they are a delight to fly. The original 'V'-Tail, that is, two tailplanes shaped like the letter 'V' and no fin, was produced just after World War II. Despite its unfortunate safety record, the aircraft quickly gained notoriety as the favoured transport of well-heeled professionals. Today it is still burdened with the nickname 'the fork-tailed doctor killer'. Buddy Holly, the famous musician, died in one, hence the song 'The day the music died'.

I have flown all variants, the B33, V35 and A36 and all of them are beautiful aircraft to operate. The main issue with the accident rate is non-instrument-rated pilots suffering disorientation in cloud. These higher performance singles require a higher level of instrument skills if not an instrument rating. Poor fuel management seems to be another failing and any aeroplane requires a level of recency and proficiency. They are not cars with wings and many pilots have died proving this point.

The Piper singles tend to be more modest performers apart from the PA24 Commanche. The Commanche has a laminar flow wing section that gives the aircraft a solid feel, especially in turbulence due to its higher wing loading. During approach and landing they had to be flown accurately, too slow and they would drop out of the sky and too fast they would float forever. Once understood, a nice aeroplane to fly with a good head of speed.

In regard to bush flying, nothing beats a Cessna, especially the tail draggers, C180 and the C185. The C206 is the outback flying jeep, ruggedly built and capable of lifting high loads out of short dirt strips. Armed with big powerful trailing edge flaps, they could be a handful during a go-around with the large trim forces required. All in all, the Cessna is the one for the farm.

Homebuilt kit aeroplanes I have tended to avoid but I have flown several versions of the Jabiru and also the Vans RV6. The RV6 is a little pocket rocket but I was surprised to see it has no stall warning device. Not only that, it gives little warning of the stall in the way of airframe buffet and with any power and flap likes to drop the left wing smartly. The saving grace appears to be that most owners know what they are doing as many are retired professional pilots.

Some other interesting types have come my way including the Russian Yak52 with its incredible rate of roll. In the opposite direction, the Fletcher FU24 is an agricultural aeroplane with a surprisingly poor rate of roll. The Republic Sea Bee amphibian has its dual ignition, consisting of a car coil on one side and a magneto on the other. A ground adjustable propeller adds to the intrigue! The American trainers AA-1 and AA-5 are also interesting, where the main spars are hollow and combined as a fuel tank. Get one in a spin, the fuel sloshes to the wing tips making them impossible to recover. The Rockwell singles, the RC112 and 114, were another American attempt to design a car-like cockpit. Lacklustre performance but nice to land with their trailing link undercarriage. In summary, variety is the spice of life but in aviation you need to do your homework before launching into the sky and know your aeroplane.

The light twins are even more interesting but sadly have been the main victims of the public liability fiasco. By design certification, light twin-engine aircraft do not have the performance protections found on heavy aircraft. (The boundary between 'heavy' and 'light' is 5,700kg.) Heavy aircraft have what is known as the 'Four Segments of Performance', each stage of flight or segment must meet a minimum climb gradient following an engine failure. This is fine-tuned to cater for two, three and four engine aircraft.

Light aircraft, on the other hand, are only required to meet a 1 per cent gross climb gradient up to 5,000 feet on a standard (ISA) day. A light twin on a hot day at maximum weight may not climb at all if an engine is lost. Once these limitations are understood and considered, the aircraft can be operated safely but never with the safety margins of a passenger jet airliner.

In some ways the manufacturers are their own worst enemy, trying to be everything to everybody. Some light twins only give you the choice of full fuel or full passengers, not both. Performance compromises can be easily exceeded either deliberately or through carelessness, placing the aircraft into dangerous areas of vulnerability. Higher-powered engines, especially the geared or turbocharged ones, require correct engine handling, especially in leaning fuel mixture correctly with any gain in altitude. As you fly higher, the air is less dense so in a piston aircraft the fuel:air mixture becomes too rich. Using a mixture lever similar to a throttle, the pilot can mechanically retard the lever to restore the correct fuel:air ratio.

In pure handling qualities, Beechcraft wins again with the Beechcraft Baron but they are not my favourite. I find they are a little cramped and I have never liked their control column design. The Piper Navajo is far roomier but not as nice to fly. When empty, they are nose-heavy and have an oddly designed flight control system where the ailerons are spring-connected to the rudder. Supposedly this makes the aircraft easier to fly but I have never figured out how they came to that conclusion. During cross-wind landings you can feel the spring tension fighting against you. The Piper Seneca 1 is the worst handling of all the light twins I have flown. Empty you must have the strength of Arnold Schwarzenegger to hold the nose wheel off during landing. The rate of roll is appallingly slow due to undersized ailerons for the span. Everybody tells me the subsequent Seneca 2 and 3 are vastly superior but I have only flown the Seneca 1. A dog of an aeroplane. It reminds me of the famous English test pilot Eric 'Winkle' Brown who once wrote on a test report, "This aircraft is difficult to get into, it should be made impossible."

All the Cessna piston twins were nice to fly but some of them had overly complicated fuel systems. An hour had to be used out of the main tanks before using the auxiliaries, or the overflow would be dumped overboard and the locker tanks (if fitted) had another set of rules. A total of six tanks for two engines is not uncommon. No big deal I suppose, but people seemed to make a hash of it at times.

Overall, I have enjoyed my light twin flying – I love the freedom of single pilot operations and enjoy the uncomplicated outback airports sans all the mind-numbing rules and procedures so loved by major airports. Some of the best flying available is bush-bashing in a light twin.

ACKNOWLEDGEMENTS

Many people have helped me in writing this book, both with advice and critical acclaim.

Eric Angles, Gayle Bengston and Paul Loveday read an early draft and offered help in layout and content.

Thanks to Captain Ken Broomhead for his kind foreword. Ken was my boss for many years and a better one would be hard to find.

Captain Seb Murray of Texel Aviation read the early draft and made sure I stayed humble.

Thanks to Bob Livingston, President of the Queensland branch of the Aviation Historical Society (AHSA), for his guidance and proof-reading for historical accuracy.

I'm grateful to Captain David Maddern, recently retired A380 Captain for Emirates, for his suggestions and proof-reading. David, together with his wife Jan, was tragically killed in a light aircraft accident only days after returning the manuscript.

Thank you to Rob Finlayson, the well-known aviation photographer, for allowing me use of his excellent photos. And to David Carter for the use of his wonderful photographs.

Finally, a big thank-you to Michael Hanrahan, Anna Clemann and Karen Comer of Publish Central. Karen showed great patience in untangling the technical jargon so a layman could understand 'pilot talk'.

George
20 June 2024

AVIATION DEFINITIONS

Advanced manoeuvring. Aircraft manoeuvres outside the normal flight envelope, for example, aerobatics or stalling.

Aerial. A radio mast or wire for radio reception or navigation aid reception.

Aerodynamics. The interaction of moving objects with the atmosphere.

Aft limit. The most rearward position of the centre of gravity.

Ailerons. A hinged flight control surface, usually forming part of the trailing (rear) edge of each wing of a fixed wing aircraft. They are used to control movement around the longitudinal axis of the plane. Moving around the axis is called 'rolling' or banking'.

Airfoil or aerofoil. Curved surface designed to give lift such as aircraft wings, tails and propellers.

Airframe. Mechanical structure of an aircraft including the fuselage, undercarriage, empennage (tail structure) and wings. Excludes propulsion systems.

Airspeed. The speed of an aircraft relative to the air it is flying through.

Angle of attack. The angle a chord of an aircraft's wing meets the relative airflow. The chord is a straight line from the leading edge to the trailing edge.

ATIS. Automatic Terminal Information Service. Broadcasts actual weather conditions.

Autopilot. A device that automatically steers an aircraft, ship or spacecraft without human involvement.

Auxiliary Power Unit. The APU is self-contained and serves as an independent power source, separate from the main engines, providing power while the aircraft is on the ground and during some parts of the flight.

Ballast. Weight other than payload to balance an aircraft.

Base-checks. Flight examination to test a pilot in abnormal and emergency operation.

Battery cart connection. Plug connection to an aircraft for an external electrical source.

Bi-planes. Fixed wing aircraft with two main wings stacked above each other.

BOBCAT. Bay of Bengal Crossing Arrival Time.

By-pass engines. A jet engine producing thrust using a combination of jet core efflux and bypass air which has been accelerated by a ducted fan, driven by the jet core.

Camber. The curve in the top surface of a wing or airfoil.

Canopy. The transparent 'bubble' enclosure over the cockpit.

Captain. Pilot in command.

CFI. Chief Flying Instructor.

Chip detectors. Magnetic Chip Detectors (MCDs) are devices used to detect metal shavings or particles in engine lubrication systems.

Circuits and bumps. A manoeuvre used when learning to fly fixed wing craft. It involves landing on a runway and taking off again without coming to a complete stop.

Cleats. Flight control locks to prevent movement by wind action on a parked or stationary aircraft.

Coffin corner. A point at high altitude where the low-speed limit (stall) and the high-speed limit (Mach buffet) come together.

Control column. Pilot's principal control wheel or stick to operate the aircraft.

Control tower. Elevated tower for air-traffic controllers to observe and direct aircraft in the vicinity of the aerodrome for take-offs, landings and safe and organised approaches.

Coupled piston engines. Two engines geared to drive one propeller shaft.

Data card. A card to record take-off and landing performance data for quick reference.

Decompression. Uncontrolled drop in pressure of a sealed system where the inside pressure drops to the outside value.

Electronic Engine Control. Controls the fuel supply, air management fuel injection and ignition.

Elevator. Primary flight control about the lateral axis. Refer to Pitch (raise and lower the nose).

Engine Nacelles. The protective housing of the engine.

Epaulets. Shoulder decorations denoting rank. Captain – four bars, Senior F/O – three bars, F/O – two bars.

F/O. First Officer or Co-pilot.

Fairings. Panels covering external parts.

Flare. The point where the nose is raised during the landing just prior to touch down.

Flat spin. A flat spin can be caused by the centre of gravity being too far aft. The wings of the aircraft descend in tight circles remaining almost horizontal.

Flight level change (FLCH). An auto pilot mode used to climb or descend.

Flight plan. A flight plan is a document which provides specified information to air traffic service units relative to an intended flight or portion of a flight.

Flutter. Self-activated vibration under the interaction of the inertial force, aerodynamic force of the structure. Can be destructive.

Fly-by-wire flight controls. Replaces the conventional operation of an aeroplane's controls by cables and hydraulics to electronic signals from a computer.

Flying block. An individual pilot roster.

Freeze period. Period where a pilot cannot bid for a change in type or promotion under the employment agreement.

Fuel check. Fuel total and fuel added is cross-checked on every flight.

Fuselage. The main body of the aircraft holding crew, passengers and cargo.

G. See load factor.

Gear sequence. The sequence of undercarriage retraction, including all door components.

General Aviation. Defined by ICAO as "all civil aviation operations other than scheduled air services and non-schedules air transport operation for renumeration or hire."

Ground-loop. Directional loss of control on the ground.

Gyroscopic. The tendency of a rotating object to maintain its direction of rotation.

Heat turbulence. Isolated convective currents caused by warm air rising.

HF aerial. High Frequency aerial.

High-lift devices. Normally refers to flaps and slats designed to create extra lift for slow speed flight.

Hypoxia. When the body doesn't receive enough oxygen.

IFR. Flight by Instrument Flight Rules.

ILS. Instrument Landing System.

Initial command check-outs. Flight tests for new Captains.

Instrument flying. Flying with reference to internal instrumentation only.

Instrument rating. Allows a pilot to fly by instrument only after a course of training.

International standard atmosphere. Base reference atmosphere of Sea Level Temp 15 degrees Celsius pressure 1013 mb.

Leg for leg. A sector, or one take-off and one landing.

Load factor. Load factor is measured in units referred to as 'G'. A unit of force. G-Force is an expression of how much your body will appear to weigh with a rapid change of position.

Logbook. A pilot logbook is a record of a pilot's flying hours. It contains every flight flown, including flight time, and types of instrument approaches made.

Low pitch lock and one high pitch lock. Propeller protection devices to prevent a runaway propeller.

Mach .85. Mach number is the ratio of the velocity of a fluid to the velocity of sound in that fluid. .85 is 85 per cent of the speed of sound. Mach 1 is the speed of sound and at sea level is around 761 mph.

Manual load sheet. A weight and balance calculation which includes trim and flap settings.

Mercy flight. Medical emergency where the pilot in command is given a higher level of flexibility and priority.

Minimum Dry Power. Min Dry PWR – Power derived from a turboprop engine without water methanol. (Water methanol is used to lower critical internal temperatures, thus allowing more power.)

Minimum Torque. Min TQE – the minimum power for given weight and temperatures to meet aircraft performance.

Mixtures. The ratio of fuel and air.

Monoplanes. Fixed wing aircraft with a single pair of wings.

Multi-engine engine experience. In-flight hours obtained in an aircraft with more than one engine.

NATS. North Atlantic Track System. Unique to the Atlantic to handle high density traffic.

Navigation training. Training in cross country navigation.

NDB. Non-Directional Beacon – a navigational aid in the medium or low frequency range transmitting a signal in all directions.

Overshoot. When an aircraft deviates off or overruns the runway surface or abandons a landing.

Performance Data Computer System. PDCS – an early flight management system.

Piston-engine (Aviation). Piston-powered engines connected to a propeller to provide thrust.

Pitch. Movement around the lateral axis. The lateral axis is a straight line which runs from wing tip to wing tip.

Pitot. Pitot tube, device measuring dynamic and static air pressure.

Pressure. Air pressure – decreases with altitude.

Pressurisation systems. Controls the cabin pressure and exchange of air from the inside of the cabin. Maintains a lower cabin altitude inside the cabin at high altitudes.

Primers. Control to prime the piston engine prior to start.

Propeller. Mechanical device with two or more blades that spin around a shaft to produce thrust.

Propeller pitch. Ability to change the angle of a propeller blade for greater efficiency.

Radial engine. An engine with the cylinders radiating out from a central crankcase.

Radio navigation aid. Ground radio beacons transmitting bearing or distance to aid navigation.

Relief captain. Used when duty limits require two crew on a long-haul flight. Relieves the rostered Captain to allow rest in cruise.

Rotary engine. An engine with a fixed crankshaft and the engine and propeller rotating around it.

Route rationalisation. Reducing or removing uneconomical destinations.

Rudder. Control surface to create yaw and directional change.

Scud running. The practice of flying low under low-lying cloud. The aim is to stay clear of weather and fly visual rather than instrument flight rules.

Service ceiling. Maximum altitude capability of an aircraft.

Simulator. Training device representing accurately a real aircraft in motion.

Sink rate. Vertical descent rate.

Spin strakes. Fairings to keep the airflow active over the tail surfaces in a stall.

Spinning. Rotating nose down in a stalled condition around the normal axis.

Spiral dive. Corkscrew rapid descent.

Spoilers. Panels on the upper wing surface which can be raised to dump lift.

Stalled. A wing is stalled when the air over a wing loses it smooth laminar flow.

Standard Operating Procedures. SOP – disciplined cockpit procedures so all crew operate to the same standards of operation.

STAR. Standard Instrument Arrival.

Swept wings. Used in high-speed aircraft. Wings are usually swept backwards but can be swept forward.

Tailplanes. Flying surfaces either fixed or moveable on the aircraft's tail to control the aircraft pitch.

The leans. Aviation slang to describe spatial disorientation due to limitations in the human ear.

Three-crew cockpit. Normal reference to two pilots and a flight engineer but can mean three pilots.

Three-pointer landings. Landing a tailwheel equipped aircraft on all wheels simultaneously.

Throttle. Means of controlling thrust by movement of a lever.

Thrust management. Using the minimum amount of thrust to save wear and tear on an engine, for example, only using full power if absolutely necessary.

Torque of the spinning engine. A force that causes an opposite rotation. If a propeller turns clockwise, the torque will pull in the opposite direction (anticlockwise).

Trimmed. All control forces are removed for balanced flight.

Tropopause. The transition zone between the troposphere and the stratosphere.

Turbine-time. Flying logged on aircraft equipped with turbo prop engines.

Turboprop aircraft. One or more turbine engines are connected to a gearbox that turns the propellers.

Undercarriage. Includes wheels which support the aircraft on the ground. It can be fixed or retractable.

Vapour lock. Fuel vapouring in fuel lines due to heat.

Velocity minimum control. VMCA – minimum speed while in the air that directional control can be maintained with an engine inoperable on a multi-engine aeroplane due to asymmetric thrust.

VLF OMEGA. Very Long Frequency navigation aid.

Water Methanol Check Pressure. The pressure within the water methanol system.

Yaw. Directional change in the horizontal plane. The rudder is the primary control for yaw.

www.ingramcontent.com/pod-product-compliance
Lightning Source LLC
Chambersburg PA
CBHW030035100526
44590CB00011B/212